The
WISDE
BOOK OF HEROIC
PERFORMANCES

The WISDEN BOOK OF HEROIC PERFORMANCES
Highlights from the Eighties

Graham Otway

Stanley Paul
London   Sydney   Auckland   Johannesburg

Stanley Paul & Co Ltd

An imprint of Random Century Group Ltd
20 Vauxhall Bridge Road, London SW1V 2SA

Random Century Australia (Pty) Ltd
20 Alfred Street, Milsons Point, Sydney 2061

Random Century New Zealand Limited
PO Box 40–086, Glenfield, Auckland 10

Century Hutchinson South Africa (Pty) Ltd
PO Box 337, Bergvlei 2012, South Africa

First published 1990

© Graham Otway 1990

Set in Palatino Roman by Deltatype Ltd, Ellesmere Port

Printed and bound in Great Britain by Scotprint Ltd, Musselburgh

British Library Cataloguing in Publication Data
Otway, Graham
    The Wisden book of heroic performances.
    1. Cricket. Matches, history
    I. Title
    796.35′ 87

ISBN 0 09 174410 5

Contents

Acknowledgements

The author would like to thank Amanda Ripley for her help with the research and all the players who gave their time for interviews. He and the publishers wish to thank Patrick Eagar, Graham Morris and Adrian Murrell/AllSport for their permission to reproduce copyright photographs and the following publishers and authors for giving permission to quote extracts: Chatto & Windus for Imran Khan's *All-Round View*, Sidgwick and Jackson for Kapil Dev's Autobiography and Methuen London for Allan Border's Autobiography.

Introduction

Throughout the 1980s it seemed that barely a week passed without a Test match or, more often than not, a one-day international being played somewhere in the world. It has been an extraordinarily busy decade matched, certainly in England if not elsewhere, by an increase in publicity given to a host of talented stars.

Choosing the pick of their heroic performances has not been easy, especially when one considers the vast number of outstanding performances from players such as Viv Richards, Allan Border, Ian Botham and Richard Hadlee, to name but a few. Each of them has become a cricketing legend, producing enough runs or wickets to fill a dozen volumes.

My choice therefore has been totally arbitrary. I preferred Botham at Old Trafford in 1981 rather than the astonishing turn-around he manufactured at Headingley two Tests earlier, and had richer memories of Richards on the same Manchester ground three years later in a one-day international than of his whirlwind Test century at Antigua in 1986.

Of course, it is not only the game's superstars who produce heroics – with so much professional cricket played at all levels over ten years there have been other feats by lesser mortals which I chose to include since they, too, were heroes for at least one day.

Graham Otway

Westerham
November 1989

David Gower
Jamaica, 1981

Few twenty-one-year-olds on their Test debuts possess the calm confidence to pull their first delivery in international cricket away to the leg-side boundary, as David Gower did when he faced up to Pakistan's Liaquat Ali at Edgbaston in 1978. It was the dawn of a glittering career for the talented left-hander from Leicestershire who went on to make 58 in his first England knock. His maiden Test century followed later that summer against New Zealand at The Oval, and many thought that Gower had established his place in the England side for years to follow when, back at Edgbaston in 1979, he scored his first Test double-hundred against India.

However, the hallmark of any batsman who wishes to be considered among the world's elite is to make runs in the cauldron of the Caribbean against the pace and fire of the mighty West Indies. In Gower's case he had already appeared in twenty-five Test sides for England when he finally came of age at Sabina Park, Jamaica, where he salvaged a draw for his side with an immensely disciplined 154 not out.

By April of 1981 Clive Lloyd's blitzkrieg strategy with fast bowlers had already established the West Indies as the reigning kings of world cricket, and the forces under his command in Jamaica were formidable.

The ace in the pack was Michael Holding. At twenty-seven, the former high school athlete was at the peak of his powers. Tall and slim with the grace of a gazelle, he had earned the nickname 'Whispering Death' among umpires, who claimed they could never hear his footfall as he approached the crease to bowl. Although a mild-mannered character off the field, he was able to generate fearsome speed and awkward bounce with the ball, and by the time the two teams arrived in Kingston for the Fifth Test his reputation had already been further enhanced. During the Third Test at Barbados, Holding had opened the England innings with an over to Geoff Boycott that was simply frightening. The Yorkshireman was beaten comprehensively by four balls, managed to get the bat on a fifth, and lost his off stump to the sixth.

Hunting for scalps, Holding alone was more than capable of creating havoc in the England side, but in the 1981 West Indian side, as in others since, there were three more quick bowlers with equally awesome ability.

Standing at 6 feet 8 inches Joel Garner was one of the tallest cricketers of all time, and he used the attribute well. Although harnessing a deceptively short run, Garner bowled surprisingly fast and generated considerable bounce by releasing the ball from something like ten feet above the ground, and his ability both to cut and to swing the ball presented batsmen with a variety of problems.

Then there was Colin Croft – almost as tall, strongly built, with a powerful chest-on in-swing action that tended to crush toes. His hostility had been turned into a legend by the Australians in 1978–79 when, playing for Guyana, he had drawn a strong protest from their tour manager as he struck one batsman on the head and fractured the jaw of another.

The final member of the quartet was something of a dark horse in Jamaica but within ten years he was to establish himself among the greatest fast bowlers of all time. Until that final game of the series the West Indies had employed Andy Roberts, but he had failed to get a wicket in the previous Test in Antigua and so Malcolm Marshall, a twenty-three-year-old from Barbados, was recalled.

These, then, were the credentials of the opposition Gower had to overcome, and the significance of his innings is further enhanced by events that occurred in the few weeks leading up to the Jamaica clash. England's morale had been severely undermined by losing the Tests at Barbados and Trinidad; the original tour party had lost the services of Brian Rose with eyesight trouble and Bob Willis with recurring knee problems; the Guyana Test had been called off after the state government had deported Robin Jackman because of his South African connections; and, most devastating of all, the tour's assistant manager, Ken Barrington, a father-figure to most of the players, had died of a heart attack.

The England players were forewarned that the Sabina Park pitch was likely to be the fastest they had ever encountered, on the tour during the week preceding the Test when they took on the Jamaica Island side. With Holding resting in preparation for the Test the Island side lacked a fast bowler of international class, and yet the Jamaican pacemen had still managed to cause a fair degree of trouble to all the tourists' batsmen.

David Gower cover driving Michael Holding during his defiant innings at Kingston

It was with some trepidation, therefore, that Graham Gooch and Geoff Boycott opened the England innings after Clive Lloyd had ended a sequence of losing three tosses to Ian Botham and asked the visitors to bat first. That England managed to score 285 in their first innings was almost entirely due to Gooch who, after sharing a partnership of 95 for the first wicket with Boycott, held the innings together with a brilliant 153 as his partners came and went in a regular procession. Gower's contribution to that total was just 22 before he was bowled behind his legs by Croft.

The pace and bounce which Holding extracted from the wicket while taking five for 56 gave England some cause for hope if their own fast bowler Graham Dilley could achieve the same. But the twenty-one-year-old from Kent suffered boot trouble half-way through his fourth over, and by the time emergency repairs had been carried out in the dressing room much of the shine and hardness from the ball had gone and the West Indian batsmen were settled in for a sizeable total.

Openers Gordon Greenidge and Desmond Haynes put on 116, and while England were more than content to see the backs of Viv Richards and Everton Mattis relatively cheaply, their fate appeared to be settled by Lloyd and Larry Gomes who scored 95 and 90 respectively as the West Indies compiled 442 for a more than healthy lead of 157 as the game broke up for a rest day.

England's second innings began on the fourth morning, and within an hour defeat looked inevitable. Gooch fell early, caught at first slip by Lloyd as Marshall managed to coax extra lift from the pitch, and Bill Athey fell to Holding from a delivery which did not get up quite as high as he had expected.

Within minutes of Gower arriving at the crease, England were in dire straights at 32 for 3 when Boycott departed for 12 caught in the gully off Croft. Defeat inside four days began to look inevitable, and Gower had a fortunate escape when Lloyd decided to dispense with pace and introduce the gentle off-breaks of Viv Richards. His first ball was short and wide and Gower aimed at the cover boundary only to get an edge. Lloyd at first slip was probably still thinking about his field placings; he seemed taken by surprise, and downed the chance.

Gower, however, had little to do with the tide turning away from the West Indians as the sting was taken out of their early hostility by Peter Willey who, in a vigorous attack on Croft, raced to 59 in only 55 minutes before lunch. Hopes of survival rose further as light drizzle caused the loss of three hours' play during the afternoon and with the news from the home dressing room that Marshall, who had bowled just 5 overs earlier in the day, was suffering from a strained rib muscle and would take no further part in the match.

Although Gower had reached 70 by the end of the fourth day and his partnership with Willey was worth 102, England still required a further 23 to make the West Indies bat again, and a full day's play against the Caribbean pace menace can take an awful lot of surviving in cricketing terms.

By the time Gower had scored the extra 30 runs he needed on the final morning to reach his century England had already lost the services of Willey and Roland Butcher, and soon after he had passed the landmark skipper Botham was caught in the gully. The second new ball had just been taken, England were only 58 runs ahead and there were still over three hours of the match remaining.

Gower's one hope of turning his hundred into a match-saving effort, as Holding proceeded to bowl at his nastiest, lay with wicket-keeper Paul Downton who was greeted at the crease by a barrage of short deliveries. But the pair weathered the storm, as a flawless Gower made the West Indies pay dearly for Lloyd's second-long lapse of concentration on the fourth day.

The draw was already in the bag by the final over of the match when Gower took a single off the bowling of Gomes to take his score to 154, one run ahead of Gooch's first-innings total and therefore England's highest Test knock of the series. Gower had batted for a shade under eight hours, almost identical to the length of time he had spent at the crease during his first innings of the tour some three months earlier when he had taken 187 off the President's Young West Indies XI in Trinidad. That first effort, however, had been in a warm- up game, whereas in Jamaica Gower's technique and concentration had been tested at the highest level by the most feared attack in the world. The best testimony to his 154 came from Holding, who said later:

David's was a very brave knock given the situation the match was in. I had been playing against him since 1976 and from very early on knew that we had to concentrate on bowling at his off stump. It was always a policy to give more than a fair share of short-pitched balls as well, but in Jamaica he took the lot.

Although Malcolm Marshall had only just come into our side and failed to complete the match, it was still one of the quickest West Indian attacks I had played in, with Croft and Garner completing the assault. But David played us wonderfully. Although he gave that early chance off Viv Richards, against us pacemen he never gave a hint of a chance and furthermore the ball was never going off the edge in the direction of slip or gully – it just kept finding the middle of the bat.

Gower played that historic innings to earn England a draw early in April 1981. To put its significance into perspective it is worth recording that it was to take another three series both at home and away and a total of ten successive Test defeats before England achieved another stalemate against the West Indies at Trent Bridge, Nottingham, at the start of the 1988 season.

David Bairstow
Benson & Hedges Cup, 1981

Before the facilities at the county ground in Derby were substantially updated, it could be the most desolate of places in which to play cricket. Formerly part of a racecourse, it was open to the elements with spartan facilities for spectators. It was at its bleakest early in May 1981 when Yorkshire were due to play Derbyshire in a Benson and Hedges Cup qualifying match – wet and cold – and the form of the two teams involved was little better.

Both sides had been riddled with captaincy problems for several years, and understandably the public shied away from a game that held little appeal. But for twenty-three-year-old Mark Johnson, a fast bowler from Holmfirth in the Yorkshire League, it was a big occasion – his debut in the competition – and he was to have a major impact on the game.

During the spells of play allowed by the dank Saturday weather, Derbyshire batted first and with South African Peter Kirsten scoring 65 they were well satisfied with their 202 for 8. In 4 overs before bad light meant that both teams would have to return for more on the Monday morning, Yorkshire made a cautious 12 without loss in reply.

Derby was again deserted when play resumed, and with Yorkshire losing quick early wickets it was widely assumed that the day's headlines would be dominated by a moment of controversy rather than the play itself. Having spotted that Derbyshire had only three instead of the required four fielders inside the 30-yard fielding ring, Yorkshire skipper Chris Old swung wildly at a ball from Barry Wood and was bowled. When no cry of 'no ball' was heard from either umpire, Old stormed back to the pavilion and contacted Lord's, who after a ten-minute delay agreed he should be reinstated at the crease. It appeared to matter little, however, as Old lasted only 4 more overs, adding 3 runs, before becoming another statistic in a collapse that reduced Yorkshire to 123 for 9.

It was at that stage that Yorkshire's last man, Johnson, having bowled 11 tidy overs in which he conceded just 33 runs, appeared at the crease to join David Bairstow in one of the most remarkable fight-backs ever seen in one-day cricket.

Derbyshire were fiddling through the role of fifth bowler, sharing the duties between the England off-spinner Geoff Miller and the rarely seen slow left arm of David Steele. But Bairstow slaughtered them both with a series of huge sixes, particularly against Steele as the red-haired wicket-keeper produced one over for the scorebook which read 6,4,2,2,6,6. By the time Miller, as Derbyshire skipper, accepted responsibility to bowl the 44th over, only 7 runs were needed for Yorkshire to win, and Bairstow hit him over mid-wicket for another six to put the issue beyond doubt.

Bairstow had scored 103 not out with nine sixes and three fours, and had produced a new record last-wicket stand of 80 with Johnson for the Benson and Hedges Cup.

The youngster's contribution was just 4 not out, but without his courageous defiance while Bairstow was cutting loose, Yorkshire would not have qualified for the quarter-finals. It cut little ice, however, with the committee as he was released from the county staff at the end of the season – but he had one golden memory to take with him.

Bob Willis
Headingley, 1981

When Bob Willis failed a fitness test on his right knee in Trinidad half-way through February 1981 and was forced to return home early from England's tour to the West Indies, it was on the cards that a magnificent fast-bowling career had reached a premature end. The strain of pounding his 6 foot 5 inch frame into the crease day in and day out for more than eleven years for Surrey, Warwickshire and England appeared to have taken its toll, and Willis looked destined for the dole queue.

He was no stranger to injury since in 1975 he had faced operations on both knees and against all the odds had forced his way back to the top, but at the age of thirty-one the chances of a second miraculous recovery were slim. Yet within a matter of four months Willis was not only playing cricket again but back in the England side, taking part in an astounding victory over Australia that was to enter the history

Bob Willis flying down the hill at Leeds

books and become a topic of pub conversations between cricket-lovers for years afterwards.

The secret of his rapid recovery was medical science. For many years sportsmen afflicted with knee cartilage problems had resigned themselves to painful operations, followed by weeks on crutches and then months of rehabilitation while their legs regained their strength. But by the early eighties a revolutionary technique called arthroscopy had been perfected which cut down the recovery time from months to weeks, and Willis was to become a major advertisement for its success.

Known commonly as 'keyhole surgery', arthroscopy involves the insertion of a minute hollow tube into the injured part of the body through which surgeons insert even smaller instruments to perform their operations. Rather than leaving the patient with ripped muscle tissue and scars measuring several inches across, all that remains after the operation is a small hole little bigger than a fleabite which heals quickly, and in the case of a knee operation the patient is back on their feet within days.

Willis underwent keyhole surgery within hours of his return from the Caribbean, was able to report back for early-season training with Warwickshire while England were still completing the Test series in the West Indies, and completed a remarkable comeback when called into the first Prudential Trophy side to face the Australians in a one-day international at Lord's on 4 June.

Within a month Willis was to play a key part in England's astonishing win in the Third Test match at Headingley. Although cricket's historians have long since labelled the match as Ian Botham's finest hour – the legendary all-rounder produced so many epic performances that he could fill a book by himself – Willis, in a ninety-Test career that yielded 325 wickets, never bettered his bowling performance on the final day which sent a shell-shocked Australian side plunging to defeat by 18 runs.

Ironically England's premier fast bowler of the time almost missed the match after contracting a cold during the Second Test at Lord's and having been advised to miss Warwickshire's two following County Championship games. As a result, when the selectors met on the Friday before the Leeds game was due to start to pick the England twelve, Willis's name was omitted. It was only reinstated twenty-four hours later when the bowler managed to convince Alec Bedser,

England celebrate as Geoff Lawson is caught behind by Bob Taylor

the chairman of selectors, over the phone that he expected to recover by the following Thursday and an invitation to Mike Hendrick to play was withdrawn before it reached the Derbyshire seamer.

There had been plenty of drama already in the Ashes series that summer, with England losing the First Test at Trent Bridge by four wickets and drawing at Lord's in a match which saw Botham bag a 'pair' and resign the captaincy just as Bedser, with the agreement of his co-selectors, was about to sack him. In what was seen as a desperate move England recalled the astute Mike Brearley as captain for Leeds, even though the Middlesex batsman had made it clear much earlier that he would not want to tour with England in India the following winter.

Brearley's first day back in charge was not an overwhelming success as he watched the Australians, after Kim Hughes had won the toss, progress to 203 for 3, mainly through the efforts of John Dyson, the stolid New South Wales opener, who made 102 to record his maiden Test century, while England's fielders downed three important catches.

19

For much of the second day on a wicket of fairly unpredictable bounce, the Australians consolidated with Hughes scoring 89 and Graham Yallop 58 – pretty uninteresting stuff compared with the electric action that was to follow after the weekend. It was only after tea when Botham took five for 35 that England clawed their way back into the match and persuaded Hughes to declare at 401 for 9, leaving the home openers to face two awkward overs before the close of play. The Australians were happy with their position, as Hughes later told a press conference: 'Four hundred was worth about a thousand on this pitch.'

On Saturday, the third day, it was to prove an astute judgement as the Australians, using only three seamers – the vastly experienced Dennis Lillee alongside youngsters Terry Alderman and Geoff Lawson – bowled England out in overcast conditions for 174 in just 50.5 overs. Botham offered the only spirited resistance with a quickfire 50, and when the follow-on was enforced England quickly lost Graham Gooch for a duck beautifully caught at slip by Alderman off Lillee's bowling. And England might have approached the Sunday off in an even worse position had not bad light robbed the tourists of Saturday's final hour in the field.

The twenty-four-hour break from action allowed the Australian bowlers time to recharge their batteries, and Monday morning brought a series of disasters for England. As wickets crashed, Ladbrokes from their tent on the ground offered staggering odds of 500 to 1 against an England victory in a two-horse race, and journalists and officials hastily booked out of their hotels in preparation for a finish inside four days.

It is well recorded how the match turned upside down through an innings of tremendous courage and power from Ian Botham, with significant support from tail-enders Graham Dilley and Chris Old. On his way to 149 not out Botham shared stands of 117 for the eighth wicket with Dilley, who made a career best 58, and 67 with Old. But when on the fifth morning the Australians finally ended England's resistance as Willis fell to Alderman, England's lead was only 129 and there were over five and a half hours of the match remaining.

Only once before in the entire history of Test cricket had a side that had been forced to follow on emerged triumphant, and as Botham and Dilley took the new ball for England there seemed little chance of success, especially when the Kent youngster had to leave the field after 2 overs to seek treatment on a thigh strain. Although Botham claimed the early wicket of Graeme Wood, there was little hint of heroics from Willis as he bowled 5 overs up the hill from the Leeds football stand end without success.

It was Willis himself who suggested to Brearley that a change of ends to allow him to steam in down the Headingley slope with the wind at his back might make a difference, and when the captain bowed to his bowler's judgement it was to prove the correct decision. With Old bowling tightly up the hill and conceding only 11 runs in 8 niggardly overs, Willis, his knee creaking and arms flailing like a goose in a flap – hence his nickname – roared in to bowl England to victory.

He began his historic rout of the Australians with a sharp, straight bouncer to Trevor Chappell which the younger brother of the two former Aussie skippers could only lob into the hands of wicket-keeper Bob Taylor as he desperately tried to protect his face. Old unsettled Dyson by twice striking him painful blows on the hands in one over, and with lunch only minutes away Willis struck again, having Hughes well taken at third slip by Botham moving to his left. By the time the interval arrived the Australians were in even deeper trouble at 58 for 4 as Yallop could only deflect another kicking Willis delivery into the hands of Mike Gatting at short square leg.

Brearley's orders to Willis had been succinct: 'Bowl short and straight' – adding that he should not worry about no-balling as he stretched for extra pace. After the interval, however, it was Old who produced the next significant breakthrough as Allan Border's leg stump was sent cartwheeling. The game built up in a magnificent crescendo and Dyson, who had spent over two hours making 34 while wickets fell at the other end and had just hooked Willis for four, attempted to repeat the shot and merely gloved a catch behind.

Completing a devastating spell of six wickets in 6 overs, Willis also induced a rash hook from Rod Marsh which required a well-judged catch on the deep fine-leg boundary by Dilley, and after being warned for too many short deliveries he found the edge of Lawson's bat to give Taylor a third catch. But an extraordinary match was by no means over.

In 4 overs of mayhem Lillee and Ray Bright launched an Australian counter-attack that yielded 35 runs to take the Australians to within 20 of victory. But Willis intervened as Lillee mistimed his drive at a half-volley, and Gatting, moving in at mid-on, lunged forward to complete his second good catch of the innings. Then England's heart missed two beats in quick succession. Ian Botham had asked especially for a third slip against Bright but then watched in agony as Old, normally one of the safest pair of hands in that area, spilled two half-chances. In the end it mattered not, however, as Willis summoned up enough energy for a tenth successive over in which he bowled a middle-stump yorker that beat Bright to close the Australian innings on the superstitiously ominous total of 111.

England had won a memorable game by 18 runs, and Willis had carved himself a niche in history with figures of eight for 43. As Brearley later wrote: 'Bob Willis had come back from the borders of oblivion to set the Ashes alight.'

Ian Botham
Old Trafford, 1981

In terms of pure powerful big hitting, Gilbert Jessop, who played for Gloucestershire for twenty years either side of the turn of the century and appeared in eighteen Tests for England, became a legend. His reputation, which far outgrew his slight 5 foot 7 inch frame, was founded at The Oval in 1902 when, as England slumped to 48 for 5 while chasing 263 to beat the Australians, he scored 100 in 57 minutes off only seventy-five balls to set up an historic one-wicket victory. To this day it remains the fastest Test century, measured by the yardsticks of both minutes and deliveries, ever scored in a Test by an Englishman. Furthermore, it was achieved at a time when the regulations stated that for a shot to be counted as six the ball had to be struck clean out of the ground and not merely over the perimeter of the playing area.

Although this book deals primarily with heroic feats from the 1980s, that potted history is vital to put into context the words of John Woodcock, who was cricket correspondent for *The Times* for more than thirty years, when as editor of *Wisden* he wrote in 1982:

> No-one, I believe, can ever have played a finer Test innings of its type than Botham's at Old Trafford. I have been told that Australia's attack was by no means one of their strongest and that by the time Botham came in the best of their bowlers, Lillee and Alderman, were on their last legs. To which I will only say that you would never have known it from the way they were bowling. At Headingley and Old Trafford we witnessed the reincarnation of Gilbert Jessop.

In the summer of 1981 Ian Botham, judged by all that he had achieved before and all that was to follow later, was at his peak as a world-class all-rounder. By the time he faced up to that summer's Australians, led by Kim Hughes, he had already achieved thirteen five-wicket Test hauls with his fast-medium swing bowling and scored six centuries for England, besides proving an exceedingly athletic slip fielder with lightning-fast reactions.

He had already inspired banner headlines on numerous occasions – at Lord's in 1978 against Pakistan and playing in only his seventh

Test he became the first player in history to score 100 and take eight wickets in an innings of the same match; he had scored 114 and taken thirteen wickets against India at Bombay in the Golden Jubilee Test of 1980; he had become the fastest player in history to achieve the all-rounder's Test double of 1000 runs and 100 wickets, needing only twenty-one Tests; and he had required the shortest time (4 years 126 days) to reach 2000 runs and 200 wickets. Botham had been rewriting the record books for five years by 1981 and had become the delight of cricket's statisticians and the darling of English crowds, who spilled out of bars the moment it was announced he was either starting to bowl or arriving at the crease to bat.

By the time England and Australia arrived at Manchester for the Fifth Test in the second week of August, English cricket was already buzzing with fresh admiration for the man. Having resigned the England captaincy after the Second Test at Lord's, he had bounced back to turn the Headingley Test on its head with a brilliant 149 not out, and then bowled England to victory at Edgbaston with a devastating spell of five for 1 in twenty-eight deliveries just when the tourists looked set fair to sail past a victory target of 142. In almost any other era of the game either of those two performances would have richly deserved a chapter of their own. But even they were eclipsed by the sheer majesty of Botham's 118 in England's second innings at Manchester which set up a 103-run victory, the side's third on the trot, to ensure that the Ashes stayed on home soil.

Despite the shock of losing the previous two Tests when the champagne to celebrate victory had long before been put on ice, the Australians' spirit, after Hughes won the toss and opted to bowl first on a damp wicket in overcast conditions, had recovered sufficiently for them to enjoy the upper hand on the opening day. Dennis Lillee and Terry Alderman had the experience to exploit the conditions ruthlessly, and they received ample support from Mike Whitney, an unknown twenty-two-year-old paceman from Sydney. He had originally intended to spend the summer gaining knowledge in the Northern League, where his potential was spotted by Gloucestershire. But he had played only two Championship games when the night before the Test he was plucked from obscurity to make his Australian Test debut as it became known that neither Rodney Hogg nor Geoff Lawson would be fit. The trio reduced England to 175 for 9, with only Chris Tavaré putting up any resistance. The Kent right-

The full power of Ian Botham at Old Trafford

hander had been specifically recalled by the selectors to stiffen up the number-three batting position after earlier incumbents had failed to pass 50 in any of England's preceding twelve Tests. Tavaré's response was to spend four and three-quarter hours at the crease fighting his way to 69. On the second morning England reached 231 all out only through the efforts of tail-enders Bob Willis and Paul Allott, who put on 56 for the last wicket with the latter marking his Test debut in front of his home Lancashire crowd with a priceless 52 not out, which more than doubled his previous best first-class score.

The dank grey north-western skies of Thursday had given way to sunshine on the second morning and with the pitch steadily drying out the Australians, with the benefit of better conditions, had high hopes of striding past the English total to put themselves back in with a chance for the series. Graeme Wood certainly started with that intention as he hooked three fours and a six in the opening overs from Willis and Allott, but that charge came to an abrupt end as the two English pacemen reduced the Australians to 24 for 4 with the aid of two Botham catches and two favourable lbw decisions. At a time when sturdy defence was desperately called for the visitors embarked on a policy of all-out attack, and while it yielded a half-century off only forty-two deliveries for Martin Kent, England, with Willis taking four for 63, bowled them out for 130 in only 30.2 overs – the shortest Test innings by an Australian side since 1902 when they were dismissed on a drying pitch at Birmingham for 36 runs in only 23 overs.

England's second innings, beginning before tea on the second day, started badly as Graham Gooch departed early, bowled by Alderman. But when a ship needed steadying there were no better qualified sheet-anchors than Tavaré and Geoff Boycott, and by Friday's close England, at 70 for 1 and with a lead of 171, appeared to have turned the tide. The excitement stirred by the events of the previous four Tests ensured a full-house crowd at Manchester on the Saturday, but England suddenly began to rue the presence of two slow scorers at the crease. Only 34 runs were added in 2 hours 20 minutes' play and four wickets went down, despite evidence that the wicket was still showing no real signs of malice.

The total complexion of the game was altered by the arrival at the wicket of Botham when England were 205 runs ahead but by no means in total command. He began tentatively, with his first thirty

Dennis Lillee barely had time to complete his follow-through before this drive reached the boundary

balls faced yielding just three singles, and then gradually changed gear with an attack against the spinner Ray Bright that saw two fours speared through the off side.

It was the advent of the new ball which saw Botham, who had been dismissed first ball on the opening day, burst out of his shell in a murderous spell of hitting that would have flattened any attack. Dennis Lillee, knowing full well Botham's inability to resist the bouncer, set two men back on the leg side for the hook, but England's hero merely responded with three sixes in the space of 2 overs which cleared the men waiting on the boundary by many a mile.

When Lillee attempted to pitch the ball up, Botham responded with a fierce straight drive, barely six feet off the ground, which would have decapitated the bowler had he not been stooping at the end of his follow-through. In an innings of such naked aggression there were bound to be chances, but the most obvious – to Whitney running back from mid-off to try to get under a steepling skier – was by no means easy.

While Tavaré at the other end appeared to be in most danger from a series of on-drives which threatened his health as he backed up,

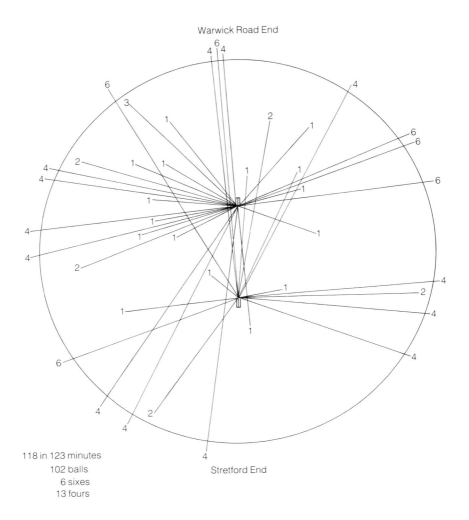

Scoring chart for Ian Botham at Old Trafford, 1981

Botham showed no mercy as he moved from 3 to 103 in just fifty-six balls, reaching three figures with yet another six and inspiring great surprise when he went at one stage for six balls without scoring a run.

The party ended only when, with 118 by his name on the scoreboard and with the Australians almost dumbstruck by his power, Botham edged Whitney into the hands of Rod Marsh. In an innings which contained six sixes and thirteen fours, few could remember a shot which did not fly directly off the middle of his 3lb

2oz bat, and while there were few boundaries struck through the area of mid-wicket, the advertising boards at deep point and extra cover took a pasting. Of the 149 Botham and Tavaré shared for the sixth wicket, the Kent man's contribution was just 28, but he had been brought back to do a specific job and scores of 69 and 78 in Manchester proved that the selectors' decision had been a wise one.

And so for the third time in as many matches Botham had turned a match upside down and England readily cashed in. Following his departure there were entertaining half-centuries from Alan Knott and John Emburey – though each paled into insignificance after the Lord Mayor's Show – and when England were finally dismissed for 404 the Australians were left with a target of 506 to win in a shade over five sessions.

Considering the pounding they had taken from Botham in the previous month, Hughes' men made a commendable effort. Batting with far more discipline than they had on the second day and with valiant centuries from Graham Yallop and Allan Border, they made 402 before they were all out only 25 minutes before the umpires were due to signal the final 20 overs of the match.

So England won by 103 runs, and a summer which had begun with Botham in charge and with a four-wicket defeat in the opening Test at Trent Bridge was drawing to a close with England in almost total ascendancy. That was due almost entirely to one man. Although, through a series of injuries and even a suspension on a drugs-related issue, Botham retained a fairly regular place in England's line-up throughout the rest of the 1980s, he has never quite recaptured the form that made him the hero of 1981 when his own superhuman efforts totally eclipsed the mere mortals who played alongside him.

Jim Griffiths
NatWest Trophy, 1981

When burly Jim Griffiths strode to the wicket with 8 overs to go in the 1981 NatWest Trophy semi-final at Northampton, the hearts of thousands of home supporters sank. Northants still needed 13 runs to beat Lancashire to reach the Lord's final, and given all previously known form that looked like 13 too many for the thirty-two-year-old number eleven batsman.

Waiting in gloomy light at the end of his long run was Michael Holding, at the time the fastest and most feared pace bowler in the world. Griffiths, on the other hand, possessed a world record that no one envied. He had once gone ten first-class innings without scoring a run, and with an average of only 2.92 during his seven-year career his chances of survival were put at nil. Yet for the next half-hour Griffiths and his partner Tim Lamb (career average 12.12) took part in the most gripping of finishes that fully justified both TV and radio commentaries running over into scheduled evening programmes.

Although they would normally have been used to bowl at the end of the innings, Lancashire's skipper Clive Lloyd decided that Holding and his England-rated partner Paul Allott should go all out for the one wicket that would seal their victory. But the faster they bowled, the more determined was Griffiths to protect his wicket and with a series of scampered singles and leg byes – each one wildly cheered by the crowd – Northants edged towards their target.

At one stage Holding tested Griffiths with a deadly accurate fast straight yorker which the tail-ender somehow dug out, and it was then that Lamb felt they might just pull off a shock. He said: 'No way under any normal circumstances would Jim have been able to keep that ball away from his stumps – but he did somehow and it was at that point that I felt God was on our side.'

The pair hung on for dear life as the tension mounted, and nerves stood on end as the last of Northants' 60 overs approached with the scores level at 186. With both sides having lost nine wickets apiece, the scorers were consulted to decide what would happen should neither a wicket fall nor a run be scored in the last over. On a count-back to 30 overs Northants would have been declared the winners,

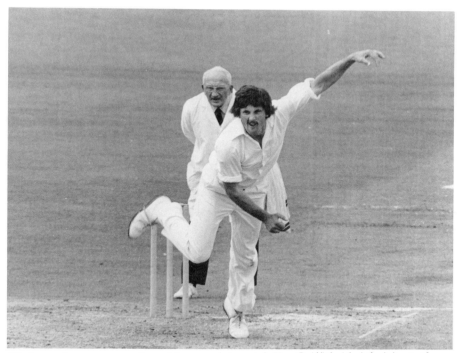

Photographers were rarely quick enough to catch Jim Griffiths' brief visits to the crease

but there was still a mountain to climb for Griffiths who had to play out six balls from left-arm spinner David Lloyd with the wicket turning. Said Lamb: 'I told Jim in no uncertain terms that he should just try and play straight to every ball, and he knew that if he got out slogging he wasn't going to be very popular.'

Griffiths duly played defensively at the first three, and off the fourth there was a massive appeal for a bat-pad catch close to the wicket, which was turned down. The fifth delivery from Lloyd gave Griffiths no chance of playing a shot. It pitched outside leg and spun viciously past the outside edge of the bat, but it also beat wicket-keeper Graeme Fowler and the batsmen were able to clinch victory with a bye.

They were mobbed by the Northants crowd and, as Lamb recalled, 'Big Jim was chaired off the field and that in itself was unique – he was given a hero's reception yet the scorebook showed he had scored 1 not out!'

Jalal-Ud-Din
Hyderabad, 1982

When Imran Khan withdrew through injury from Pakistan's side to play Australia in the first of three one-day internationals at Hyderabad in 1982, the tourists' hopes of opening the series with a victory soared. Imran's replacement was an unknown twenty-three-year-old bank employee from Karachi, Jalal-Ud-Din, whose stature on the field as a fast bowler tended to be underplayed because he wore glasses. Whatever the private thoughts of the Aussies about the newcomer, by the end of the game he had certainly left his mark.

Pakistan batted first and quickly put the Australians on the defensive as Mudassar Nazar and Mohsin Khan put on 82 for the first wicket. Mudassar went on to make 104, and even without Imran's bowling Pakistan's 229 for 6 from 40 overs was going to take some overhauling. Bruce Laird and Graeme Wood gave the Aussies a flying start with an opening stand of 104, but before another five runs had been added both openers and captain Kim Hughes were removed by off-spinner Tauseef Ahmed.

The Australians got back on course as John Dyson and Allan Border added a further 48, but then Jalal-Ud-Din struck. He opened his international account by having Border caught behind by Wasim Bari. His next over was deadly as he produced the first hat-trick in limited-overs internationals, bowling Rod Marsh, having Bruce Yardley caught behind and entering the record books by bowling Geoff Lawson.

The collapse was all too much for the Aussies who crashed to 170 all out, suffering defeat by 59 runs, and the unknown Jalal-Ud-Din was rewarded for his figures of four for 32 with his first Test cap three weeks later.

Imran Khan
Faisalabad, 1983

When Imran Khan stirred from sleep in his Karachi hotel bed on the morning of Christmas Eve 1982 he experienced a sharp new pain in his left leg. The day before he had bowled 12 overs as Pakistan had opened the second Test of the season by bowling out India for 169, but despite racking his brains he could not remember feeling discomfort at any stage on the field. And later that morning when the pain wore off during his team's pre-play exercise session, he decided to dismiss it as a slight, albeit mysterious bump.

Within two months, however, doctors were to diagnose that Imran was suffering from a stress fracture of the shin – a serious injury that was to take two years out of the glittering career of one of the world's top all-rounders. But not before he had produced two bowling performances that ranked alongside the best produced in the 1980s.

Over the festive season Imran was puzzled by this sudden pain. He said:

> I got out of bed and felt a pain in my left shin-bone. We had bowled the previous day and I had not experienced any discomfort, and I could not recall any incident on the field that might have caused it. I decided that I must have knocked my leg somehow and when I got to the ground and started warming up, the pain gradually disappeared and I forgot about it. Little did I know that it would transform my career, my life and the shape of cricket in Pakistan for the next two years.
>
> The following day as I warmed up the pain reappeared and I began to suspect that it might not be an ordinary bruise. We had dismissed India cheaply on the first day and then accumulated a large total thanks to centuries by Mudassar and Zaheer. I felt no discomfort while batting and I was at the crease for some time. With India batting again almost 300 behind, the pain reappeared when I bowled – but I had been playing non-stop cricket for many months and had had a number of niggling injuries. I still hoped that this was just one of them.

As India made a spirited response to the task of scoring 284 to avoid losing to their near neighbours and bitter rivals, with Sunil Gavaskar and Dilip Vengsarkar taking them past the hundred with only one wicket down, Imran could have taken the easy way out. Many fast bowlers in the past faced with a flat lifeless wicket and suffering from leg trouble had made their polite excuses and sloped off to find peace in the dressing room. But Imran had extra responsibilities in his role as Pakistan's captain, and in any event he was to discover the best possible anaesthetic for his ailment.

Returning to the Pakistan attack shortly after tea on the third day, he produced what has been described as the fastest and fiercest spell of fast bowling ever seen on the sub-continent, and despite the blandest of wickets he did not call upon a fielder for assistance as he ploughed his way through one of the strongest and most experienced contemporary batting line-ups in the world.

The pain in his shin must have eased at the sight of a fast in-swinger piercing its way between pad and bat to shatter Gavaskar's stumps. And in the next twenty-six balls, with a gentle cross breeze helping the movement in the air, he trapped Mohinder Amarnath lbw and in succession bowled Gundappa Viswanath, Sandeep Patil and Kapil Dev. Imran had left the Indian innings in tatters and it was only a stand of 83 between Vengsarkar and Madan Lal, with both of the Indians completing half-centuries, that prevented the game ending with two spare days unused. But Imran had a second blistering spell up his sleeve which began twenty minutes before lunch when he took the edge of Vengsarkar's bat for Wasim Bari to complete the catch. Maninder Singh was clearly lbw to the next ball, and while Dilip Doshi staved off the hat-trick, his stumps were knocked over by the first ball of Imran's next over.

These amazing bursts had presented Pakistan with victory by an innings and 86 runs, and Imran's figures of eight for 60 were only marginally short of being a career best. He had also become the first player to take ten wickets in a Test between India and Pakistan, and the margin of victory was the biggest ever in contests between the two sides. To complete a list of milestones Imran, by bowling Viswanath, had taken his 200th Test wicket in only his forth-fifth international appearance.

In the week leading up to the Third Test the Indians boosted flagging morale by winning a rain and bad-light affected one-day international at Lahore, while Imran temporarily forgot his shin problems. Recalling the Karachi victory he said later:

Appealing all-rounder Imran Khan

Naturally I was elated, both as a player and a captain. I had not mentioned the pain to anyone except Mudassar, who agreed with my theory that I must have bumped my leg. So I proceeded unconcerned to the Third Test at Faisalabad. I was then at my peak as a fast bowler; all the hard work I had put in was paying off. I felt I had never been so fit in my life and knew that I could sustain long spells of consistently fast bowling.

In the years before Mike Gatting made the venue famous and the impressive Hotel Serena was built, Faisalabad was not the most popular stopping-off point for touring cricketers – it was a grimy textile city with primitive accommodation and a dusty atmosphere that it was almost possible to cut with a knife. With fast bowlers it was particularly unpopular, since the wicket on most occasions proved to be a batsman's paradise. Yet Imran, who was to be further troubled by his shin, achieved an all-round cricketing feat that had been matched only by his arch-rival Ian Botham in the previous 106 years of Test matches.

Praying there might be a touch of early moisture in the Iqbal Stadium pitch, Imran asked India to bat first on winning the toss and his new ball partner made the gamble pay off in the second over when he bowled Arun Lal. Imran consolidated the early break-through by having Gavaskar caught behind and Vengsarkar lbw, but from 18 for 3 the Indians launched a fight-back which reflected the true character of the playing surface and also led to a most entertaining first day's cricket.

Their principal stands saw Sandeep Patil and Kapil Dev add 68 and Syed Kirmani and Madan Lal put on 122 – a new record for India against Pakistan. But each time the visitors threatened to dominate, Imran produced his own answer, dismissing Patil and Madan Lal with the aid of catches and winning lbw shouts against Kapil Dev and Kirmani. After finishing with six for 98 as India were bowled out for 372, Imran commented: 'Faisalabad is normally considered a fast bowler's graveyard, but I produced one of the best performances of my career.'

Pakistan also suffered early shocks as wicket-keeper Kirmani and Kapil Dev combined to dismiss each of the top three in the order with only 79 scored in reply, but once that early fire had been put out the home side hit back with a vengeance. They moved to within 6 runs of the Indian total with a fourth-wicket stand of 287 between Javed

Another boundary on the way to the fence at mid-on

Miandad and Zaheer and then, with the Indian bowling flagging, they surged ahead as Imran and Salim Malik cut loose.

Imran admitted afterwards that he was beginning to feel his shin once again, but no one would have guessed as he reached his half-century with a pull that sailed out of the ground and passed his century with a hooked six off Kapil. On his way to 117 Imran was particularly severe on the Indian all-rounder, taking 21 off one of his overs as he accumulated a total of five sixes and ten fours. Although Imran was out with the Pakistan total at 574, caught off the bowling of Maninder Singh, he allowed the Indians no respite. Malik batted on to become the fourth Pakistani in the innings to complete a century, and when the declaration finally arrived on the fourth day the home lead was worth 280.

India were quickly facing defeat as Sarfraz and Imran removed three of their top four batsmen inside half an hour, but Gavaskar and Amarnath batted with staunch defiance to take them to 181 for 3 by stumps, the fourth day giving hope that they could save the game. After a night's rest however, Imran ran in at full tilt on the final morning and when he sent back Amarnath, lbw for 78, Indian wickets began to fall regularly to the Pakistan pace attack. Although Gavaskar soldiered on to make 127 not out in seven hours, the game ended in a ten-wicket victory for Pakistan half an hour before tea. Imran finished with five for 82 giving him eleven wickets in a Test for the second match running, so he joined Botham (who had achieved the feat against India in the Golden Jubilee Test at Bombay in 1980) as only the second player to take ten wickets and score a century in the same Test match.

Imran proved just as devastating in the Fourth Test at Hyderabad, taking eight wickets as he led Pakistan to victory by an innings and 119 runs; and while the Fifth and Sixth Tests ended in draws, he was still the outstanding bowler in Pakistan's three–nil series win. He finished with forty wickets at a cost of 13.95, and a batting average of 61.75 was not to be sniffed at. But the valiant efforts of Pakistan's handsome national hero had taken their toll. The shin had been giving him constant problems since the Third Test, as he explained:

I could feel the pain even when batting. The ball was keeping low and because I was constantly on the front foot I was often hit on the shin; for a time I blamed the problem on sub-standard pads. Eventually I consulted a physiotherapist who said it was just a bruise. I didn't want anything to interrupt our progress in the series, so I accepted his diagnosis and went to Hyderabad for the next Test.

After this the pain got worse. A lump appeared on my shin-bone and I kept having to spray the area to dull the pain before bowling. Even so the agony was intense. I kept bowling until I had crossed the pain barrier, but as soon as I stopped I could hardly stand.

Later Imran accepted the diagnosis of X-rays taken in Lahore that revealed he had a stress fracture, but in Pakistan's interests he agreed to travel to England for the 1983 World Cup purely as a specialist batsman, a role he continued to play for Sussex in the County Championship after the competition had ended. It was a mistake, since by the end of the English summer the small stress crack in his bone had widened. Against his better judgement, and in a bid to smooth over a selection crisis, Imran also agreed to captain Pakistan in Australia, but just weeks after arriving Down Under a doctor ordered him to take two months off from the game. It was eighteen months after the original pain had appeared in his leg that Imran was finally cleared to resume cricket as an all-rounder, but he never did fully recapture those glorious days which saw him at his peak against the Indians early in 1983.

New Zealand *v.* England
Benson & Hedges Cup, 1983

England desperately needed to beat New Zealand at Adelaide in January 1983 to keep alive their chance of reaching that year's finals of the triangular Benson and Hedges Cup. And when they scored 296 for 5 from their 50 overs to set a new record for the competition, victory seemed assured. But their record lasted barely three hours.

The notoriously flat Adelaide Oval pitch had lived up to its reputation as Ian Botham, opening for England, made 65 of the first 75 runs scored and David Gower maintained the momentum with a fluent 109. Even after the left-hander's departure there were still fireworks to follow from Trevor Jesty, who struck two sixes off Gary Troup in the 50th over to give the total an invincible look.

By rights New Zealand should already have wilted, especially since the temperature was well over 100 degrees, and before their own 100 had been posted the side's three leading batsmen, Glenn Turner, John Wright and Geoff Howarth, were all back in the pavilion. But the fight-back began when the Kiwis promoted big-hitting Lance Cairns to number five and he and Jeff Crowe added 70 in only 8 overs as England suffered an epidemic of dropped catches. Richard Hadlee and Jeremy Coney then added 121 in 18 overs and when England captain Bob Willis felt enough was enough and brought his own bowling back into the front line, his first over was a nightmare, containing two leg-side wides and costing 14 runs.

That left New Zealand needing 18 from 3 overs and while Hadlee, who had scored 79 from only sixty-four balls, fell to a boundary catch by Jesty, New Zealand calmly pulled off an historic victory with four wickets and seven balls to spare.

Kapil Dev
Tunbridge Wells, 1983

A tumbler full of cold water, an empty chair and a quiet, deserted dressing room probably played as important a part as any of the fine individual performances that led to India pulling off one of the major shocks in the history of one-day cricket when they beat the West Indies to lift the World Cup in 1983.

The three strange ingredients were not in evidence at Lord's but a week earlier in India's Group B qualifying match at Tunbridge Wells against Zimbabwe. The African side had qualified for the final stages of the competition by winning the ICC Trophy in 1982, but coming from a non-Test-playing nation they were widely regarded as little more than cannon fodder in the World Cup – there simply to make up to eight the number of sides involved in the qualifying groups.

That notion, however, had been quickly smashed over the head in their opening game when Zimbabwe gave notice of their intentions

Kapil Dev showing little mercy against Zimbabwe with bat . . .

with a 13-run victory over the Australians at Trent Bridge. And although they had lost their three subsequent games, their reputation had been enhanced with a fighting, though losing, performance against the West Indies. The Indians had set out on the World Cup trail with victories over the West Indies and Zimbabwe but, following two losses, victory in their second meeting with Zimbabwe was vital. If the game was to end in defeat then at least Kapil Dev's side had to score quickly enough to give it a chance of edging the Australians out of the semi-finals on run rate.

Such calculations quickly flew out of the window after skipper Kapil Dev chose to bat first at Tunbridge Wells and found his team confronted with a lively damp pitch and two opposition bowlers with little respect for reputations. Sunil Gavaskar had been an Indian hero in many Tests during the previous decade but he had recently been out of form and was playing only because of an injury to Dilip Vengsarkar. Peter Rawson's first ball flew past his nose from just short of a length, to give Gavaskar doubts about the playing surface, and when the final ball of the opening over kept low he was plumb lbw.

Given Gavaskar's poor form it was a disappointing if not totally unexpected start, but the carnage that followed in the next dozen overs was not the sort of display considered worthy of potential world champions. Mohinder Amarnath had some excuse as Rawson produced a lethal off-cutter which he could only edge into the hands of Syed Kirmani, but Krish Srikkanth played a reckless shot at Rawson's partner Kevin Curran and was caught at mid-off, and Sandeep Patil, in the tenth over, played an airy shot at Curran and was caught behind down the leg side.

Kapil Dev was not in the best of moods when he walked to the wicket with his side 9 for 4, and only 8 more runs had been added when Yashpal Sharma nicked Rawson into the wicket-keeper's gloves. For the moment all thoughts of a large total had vanished and it became a question of whether India would survive as long as the lunch break. There was some relief as Roger Binny carefully added 60 runs with Kapil Dev. But John Traicos, the thirty-seven-year-old spinner who had once played Test cricket for South Africa, ended a nagging spell by trapping Binny lbw for 22, and the value of the partnership looked wasted an over later when Ravi Shastri played rashly at Zimbabwe's other spinner Duncan Fletcher and was caught at mid-off.

. . . and ball

Although Kapil Dev had completed a half-century, by the lunch interval the Indians had managed to stagger to only 106 for 7 and their captain was not amused. But it was during the break that his Indian team-mates pulled a master stroke which rescued the side from the brink of disaster and put them back on the road to eventual glory. Kapil explained later:

> I went in to lunch unbeaten and I was a very angry man. I had been quite annoyed at the way those at the top of the order had batted and when I walked into the dressing room I saw everyone trooping out. A glass of water had been left next to my chair, but not a soul was in the room. It is usually the custom for one of the reserves to bring the not-out batsmen's lunch into the dressing room. That day there was no sign of my lunch being brought and I had to walk up to the dining room to get it.
>
> I realised why this drama was being played. My team-mates had planned an ingenious way out of getting lip from their captain. They knew I could not possibly yell at them in public in the dining room. I appreciated their plan and their sense of humour in leaving only that glass of water, indicating that I should cool down. I was pretty cool by the time I walked out to resume my innings.

The transformation in Kapil and the course of the match was dramatic. Curran roared in after lunch and tried him with a bouncer and while Kapil mishit his intended pull, it carried over the short Tunbridge Wells outfield on to the roof of a hospitality tent. Curran mouthed an oath, Kapil egged him on to try another bouncer, and when it arrived a hook sent the ball hurtling out of the ground for another six.

In 16 overs Kapil Dev added 62 with Madan Lal, and he completed his century in the 49th over of the innings. But it was during a last-wicket partnership of 126 that Kapil Dev turned a high-class ton into an innings of memorable proportions. His own bat produced an average of 7 runs from each of the last 11 overs, and when the innings closed he had 175 not out beside his name. In all he hit six sixes and sixteen fours on his way to the highest score ever made in the World Cup, and from 17 for 5 India's total had been transformed to a match-winning 266 for 8.

Kapil Dev was understandably tired when it came to the Zimbabwe innings, and in his dual role as the side's leading strike bowler he was unable to set similar standards. Zimbabwe fought well with Curran scoring a blistering 73, but in the end they fell short of their target by 31 runs. As it turned out India beat Australia in their sixth and final qualifying match to make the semi-finals with a comfortable safety margin, and with their confidence approaching sky high they earned a place at Lord's with a six-wicket victory over host nation England at Old Trafford.

Their opponents were to be the West Indies, winners of the first two World Cup finals in 1975 and 1979 and odds on with the bookmakers to complete a hat-trick, especially since India were only fourth favourites at the start of the tournament with England and Pakistan generally regarded as better bets.

Airlines running services between London and Delhi had never experienced such a late rush for bookings, but many of the Indians who made a last-minute dash to get to London for the final were to be disappointed. Tickets had been sold out months earlier and the few that were available on the black market with a face value of £10 were being sold for £70 each. Those Indian fans who decided to cough up and join the 25,000 Lord's crowd must have felt cheated for a time after Clive Lloyd won the toss and asked India to bat first.

There was some early fire from Srikkanth, who savagely cut Joel Garner for four and then in one over from Andy Roberts produced a drive along the ground to mid-wicket followed by a hook over fine leg for six. But it was all too brief; after making 38 he fell lbw to Malcolm Marshall and the innings lost its impetus. Amarnath played with composure against the Caribbean pace menace, scoring 26, and Sandeep Patil flowered briefly with 27, but Kapil could not rediscover his Tunbridge Wells touch, falling to an attempted slog against the spin of Larry Gomes. But India's worst crime as they were bowled out for 183 was their failure to use up 5 of the 60 available overs.

If India's team-mates had pulled an inspirational stroke to stir up Kapil at Tunbridge Wells, at Lord's it was to be the captain who dragged his side up off the floor. He said: 'Did we believe then we had a chance? I told the boys as we prepared to go out to field, "We have nothing to lose. Nobody expected us to be here. It is only a matter of three hours from now. Throw yourselves at the ball and try." Anything was possible after Tunbridge Wells and I was trying to be as positive as possible when we took the field.'

The turbaned Balwindersingh Sandhu, who had earlier been hit on the head by Marshall when batting, took Kapil's lead by quickly bowling Gordon Greenidge with a big in-swinger, but that only brought Viv Richards to the wicket, carrying his bat with an air of arrogant disdain, and he was soon in murderous vein.

Richards moved into his stride with a pull off Sandhu for four, and in the next over from Kapil he brought West Indian fans to their feet with two more boundaries driven effortlessly through mid-off and mid-wicket. Kapil replaced Sandhu with Madan Lal, and with Richards crashing three more fours in his first over it appeared that the West Indies were racing to victory. Richards in fact hit seven fours on his way to 33, but his insistence on winning the match at a gallop cost him and the West Indies dearly. Madan Lal dug in a short ball which failed to rise, but Richards made no attempt to alter his intention to smash it over mid-wicket and spooned up a catch. When it was held, with some difficulty by Kapil running back towards the Lord's Grandstand, the game was transformed.

Madan Lal, who had earlier dismissed Desmond Haynes, added a third scalp when Larry Gomes fell to a smart catch by Gavaskar at slip, and India began to scent a possible victory when Clive Lloyd attempted to crash Roger Binny through the covers but succeeded only in finding Kapil at mid-off. At 76 for 5 after 25 overs the West Indies were in trouble, but most of their fast bowlers had a reputation for big hitting and the Indians had to hold their nerve. Although Jeff Dujon and Marshall added 43 runs without fuss, it was Amarnath who clinched an historic victory. At Lord's, with the boundaries square of the wicket short and exceedingly vulnerable, Amarnath's gentle medium pace, delivered off just four strides, could have proved disastrous. But his first ball, a gentle loosener, was played on to his stumps by Dujon, Marshall edged just as soft a delivery into the safe hands of Gavaskar at slip, and when umpire Dickie Bird raised his finger to give Michael Holding out lbw the West Indies had been bowled out for 140 and the Indians had clinched victory by 43 runs.

Kapil said afterwards: 'This combined performance was not a miracle. It just came from a feeling of self-belief and self-confidence. A whole new chapter had been written into the history of Indian cricket and we returned home to one of the finest receptions imaginable. We were on top of the world.'

Companies in their home country gave the Indian players luxury flats, motor cars and massive cash rewards. But little did the whole of the sub-continent know at the time that their World Cup triumph could be traced back to one strategically placed glass of water.

Martin Crowe
Wellington, 1984

The appearance on the scorecard of two larger-than life characters, Lance Cairns and Ian Botham, almost inevitably promised that the 1984 First Test between New Zealand and England at Wellington's Basin Reserve would produce fireworks. The fact that England captain Bob Willis needed only three more victims to become his country's leading Test wicket-taker of all time almost certainly meant it would be historic. And a century of infinite charm from the impish Derek Randall made it all the more memorable. Yet in the final shakedown it was a match-saving innings from a twenty-one-year-old with world-class potential as a batsman that left the deepest impression.

It was a combination of Botham and Willis that gave England the first-day honours, after New Zealand captain Geoff Howard had chosen to bat first on a wicket that was still damp after being left uncovered when a rainstorm had hit the New Zealand capital four days earlier. Botham inflicted the early damage as the left-handed John Wright misjudged the pace of a short ball which stopped on him and gave a catch to mid-on; Bruce Edgar touched a ball down the leg side to wicket-keeper Bob Taylor and Howarth drove without getting to the pitch of the ball and was caught by David Gower in the gully.

Willis began his bid to overtake Fred Trueman's tally of 308 wickets for England by bowling Martin Crowe, and by the end of the day he had also pocketed the scalps of Martin Snedden and Cairns, the latter falling to a brilliant slip catch by Mike Gatting to take his own total to 309. With Botham taking five for 59, New Zealand had every reason to be disappointed with their first-innings 219.

England's reply, begun shortly after the start of the second morning, showed little more authority. By the time the lunch interval arrived they had already lost both openers to the bowling of Cairns, and the massively built swing bowler was even more devastating during the afternoon session. Gower fell to a diving catch in the gully by Richard Hadlee, Allan Lamb nudged a catch to short leg, and Mike Gatting played across the line as England were reduced to 115 for 5.

It would have been even more perilous had Cairns, resting from his endeavours at slip, hung on to a chest-high chance offered by Botham before he had scored. It was to prove a costly miss. Botham was at his attacking best as he crashed twenty-two fours and two sixes on his way to 138 in 235 minutes. Randall's innings was entirely different. A complex and nervous character with a wide-open stance, who would insist on fidgeting with either his helmet or pads even while the bowler was in his run-up, he still managed to get his feet and bat in the right place at the right time to play some exquisite shots. For six and half hours, despite the occasional play and miss, he did not offer a chance while compiling 164, his second highest Test score. Despite their widely varying approaches to the game, Randall and Botham added 232 for the sixth wicket in three and a half hours, and England's final total of 463, reached just after tea on the third day, had a match-winning ring about it.

There were 14 hours and 35 minutes of the match remaining when the New Zealand second innings got under way. Their chances of saving the game seemed to fritter away as openers Wright and Edgar both played loose shots outside the off stump, Howarth was unluckily run out when Nick Cook deflected a straight drive on to the stumps, and Botham produced a short ball which kept wickedly low to win an lbw appeal against Jeff Crowe. The Kiwis were 165 for 4 and still 79 runs short of asking England to bat a second time.

For three years New Zealanders had been predicting great things from Martin Crowe. The younger brother of Jeff and the son of a first-class cricketer, he was still in his late teens when a string of fine performances in club cricket earned him a first-class debut with Auckland, and he was still only nineteen when he was given his first Test cap against Australia at the end of the 1981–82 season. But for all the opportunities, he still had a Test average of only 17 when the series with England began.

In the next four and three-quarter hours, however, England's bowlers were to discover why the strongly built, curly blond-haired right-hander had been compared for technique and grace to the great Australian Greg Chappell. Only 126 runs were added while Crowe was at the crease but such was his domination of the bowling that he scored exactly 100 of them, and no English bowler was shown mercy by his bat.

Upright and firm-footed at the crease, he produced three classic drives, either side of the bowler's stumps whenever spinner Nick

Martin Crowe cutting Ian Botham during his match-saving hundred at
Wellington

Cook overpitched, and when he dropped short Crowe leaned back and effortlessly cut the ball square. When Willis decided pace might unsettle the youngster, he produced a trio of off-side drives against the England captain, and against the normal variety of line and length served up by Botham Crowe produced the shot to match. Although it was an innings played under the most defensive of circumstances so clean was the hitting behind his attacking shots that his maiden Test hundred contained an unusually high percentage of boundaries – nineteen in all, producing 76 glorious runs. It was only the elation of breaking the Test-match century barrier that broke his previously unwavering concentration. In desperation, and with only four front-line bowlers included in his team, Willis offered the ball to Mike Gatting and before Crowe had even made a start towards his second hundred, the Middlesex man found the edge of the bat and Botham took a comfortable catch at slip.

The sight of the youngest member of their side turning the tables on England had an uplifting effect on the rest of the New Zealand dressing room and it extracted from all-rounder Jeremy Coney his first century for seven years in any sort of cricket. Having stood sedately at the opposite end while Crowe was at his peak, Coney took command of a rearguard action that was to save the game. Athough early on the fifth morning Cook bowled Ian Smith to reduce the home side to 402 for 8, just 168 ahead with over five hours of the game remaining, it was the last sight England had of victory.

Although the wicket began to turn slowly, Coney defied the visitors for over eight hours on the final two days, scoring 174 not out, and he finally secured the draw in a New Zealand record ninth-wicket stand of 118 with Lance Cairns – the tail-ender sprinkling a basically defensive 64 with eleven fours and a six. The pair took New Zealand through to 537 all out and there was no time left for England to launch a serious assault on a victory target of 294, the two Chrises, Tavaré and Smith, coasting through to the close at 69 for no wicket.

For his first-innings haul of five for 59 and a century, Ian Botham was made Man of the Match, though both Coney and Cairns were statistically equally well qualified. Statistics alone, however, could not do justice to the innings by Crowe, which had had the biggest impact on the game.

Viv Richards
Old Trafford, 1984

When a batsman possesses immense power, endless reserves of natural ability and the presence and charisma to entertain cricketing crowds wherever he may be, as is the case with Viv Richards, it becomes almost impossible to single out one heroic effort from all his many entries in the record books. Even at the age of seventeen as a schoolboy in Antigua he possessed that little bit extra, that something special which made him stand out among his contemporaries on the cricket field. It certainly brought him to public notice in a Leeward Islands tournament when the crowd became so incensed when he was given out caught behind that they stopped the play and berated the organisers so forcefully that the umpire's decision was over-turned. It was somewhat harsh on Richards that the action of his fans earned him a two-year ban from the game.

It was an unwelcome hiccup to a career that was to reach its height in the mid to late seventies as he rapidly emerged as the bright new batting star of West Indian cricket – a position that was fully confirmed in eight glorious months of 1976. In those months of action he amassed a record 1710 Test runs at an average of 90, against an Australian attack led by Dennis Lillee and Jeff Thomson at the peak of their careers, followed by an Indian visit to the Caribbean headed by those masters of spin Bedi, Chandrasekhar and Venkat, and finally in England where John Snow, Bob Willis and Derek Underwood provided no mean threat to his powers.

His exploits in England came as no surprise since he had joined Somerset in 1974, making 1223 runs in his first season with the county to launch a thirteen-year West Country career which, along with the presence of Ian Botham and Joel Garner, turned Taunton from a cricketing backwater into a county ground that few opponents relished visiting. All bowlers in turn wilted in the face of his fierce cover-driving and hooking when he was in full flow, and could only watch in frustration when in his quieter period Richards accumulated runs with carefully placed pushes between square leg and mid-on which still raced away to the ropes despite the apparent lack of effort.

In Richards' case, to extract one particular innings that stood head and shoulders above the rest from a distinguished career that was also to span the 1980s can only ferment fierce debate. Purists would demand that it should have been played in a Test match, which is universally held as the highest level of the game, but many modern cricket fans have been weaned on the instant excitement of the limited-overs game.

In the thick Richards folio there are persuasive arguments for looking at three particular performances. His 138 not out in the 1979 Prudential World Cup final at Lord's was a clearly defined match-winning effort, but a closer inspection reveals that England went into the game with a badly balanced and ill-equipped attack. Two years later he held the West Indies together scoring 120 not out in a first-innings total of only 249 against Pakistan at Multan, but the benefits were never fully realised since rain washed out all but 20 minutes' play on the last two days of a drawn game. His power could rarely have been seen in a more majestic innings than that he displayed in 1986 when, on his home ground at St John's in Antigua, he scored against England the fastest century, in terms of balls received, in a Test match. He needed only fifty-six deliveries, six of which were despatched over the ropes for six while seven others went for four. He celebrated reaching three figures with another six, and since the West Indies went on to win the game and complete a five–nil whitewash in the series, it was a truly great effort.

And yet for the 18,000 people who were packed into Old Trafford on 31 May in 1984 there can be few better memories of Richards, or any other master craftsman for that matter, in action. England's players assembled at Manchester for the first time since their ill-fated tour at the start of the year to New Zealand and Pakistan, which had been notable for a series of alleged scandals involving wild parties and drug-taking and during which distinguished performances on the field were more remarkable by their absence. Their opponents were starting out on a summer international schedule which they were expected to dominate, and there was much sentiment in the Old Trafford air – Clive Lloyd, a long-time favourite at Lancashire as a county player, was making his last tour of England as West Indian captain before retirement.

Despite the huge gap in the recent international records of the two sides, England had some justification for being confident that they could take the opening game in the three-match Texaco Trophy

Viv Richards pulls Derek Pringle during his one-man war against England at Old Trafford

series. After all, India had caused an upset at Lord's the previous summer by beating the West Indies in the World Cup final. The bright predictions from Bob Willis's team were also justified by the local conditions. The Manchester pitch with its reputed low bounce was expected to go a long way towards blunting the danger posed by a four-pronged West Indian attack comprising Michael Holding, Joel Garner, Eldine Baptiste and Malcolm Marshall. Furthermore, the wicket was expected to turn and while England had called up the vastly experienced off-spinner Geoff Miller for the game, the West Indies possessed no slow bowler of the same calibre, preferring to rely on Richards in his secondary role with the team.

England's early optimism proved well founded, as in the second over Desmond Haynes was run out after the West Indies had won the toss and chosen to take first dig. Home spirits rose as the irrepressible Ian Botham had the other opener Gordon Greenidge caught behind, and when Richie Richardson gave Willis a return catch the West Indies were in trouble at 43 for 3 with Richards striding to the crease.

The 'Master Blaster' began quietly and enjoyed a stroke of luck as a mistimed on-drive just cleared the field. At the other end Miller was beginning to produce the goods for England as he bowled Larry Gomes and had both Lloyd and Jeff Dujon caught off the top edge attempting to sweep. But the one wicket England so badly needed to consolidate the breakthrough was that of Richards, and it eluded them. When the West Indian had made 44 Miller drew Richards out of his crease and beat him down the legside, but David Bairstow failed to complete the stumping and England paid dearly for their policy of including a wicket-keeper/batsman ahead of better specialists with the gloves.

Nevertheless it was all-important for the West Indies that Richards should discover a partner capable of keeping him company at the crease, and at 106 for 7 with only Baptiste, Garner and Holding to follow, the prospect looked distinctly bleak.

Although Richards was beginning to move into full stride, having already struck Botham for 16 in one over, it was Baptiste who helped to steady the slide, scoring 26 while 55 was added for the eighth wicket before Bairstow made partial amends for his early mistake with a catch behind off Botham. Garner departed soon afterwards, falling to a return catch off Neil Foster, but that was the signal for Richards to play one of the greatest innings in the history of one-day cricket.

He had already made 96 when Garner's wicket fell, but in a new record one-day partnership for the last wicket of 106 with Holding he personally scored a further 93, allowing his partner to face just twenty-seven balls in the next 14 overs. At first he seemed content to take one four early in the over and then take a single near the end to protect Holding from the English bowlers, but as the West Indies' total passed 200 – which could well have been a match-winning total in itself – Richards cut loose.

Neil Foster, who was part of the English pace attack, recalled:

We became helpless and what was specially memorable was the power with which he hit the ball. I remember Derek Pringle trying to tie him down with a low full toss – in one-day cricket that normally restricts the batsman to a single and you are going well to get it away for a four. But Viv picked it up and put it out of the ground for a six over that stand at the Warwick Road End. He certainly hit me for one six straight back over my head and he did the same to Bob Willis, hitting him low and hard.

By the time the West Indies had used up all of their 55 overs, Richards had taken his score to 189 not out and his side to 272 for 9 – a total which Lloyd's four fast bowlers were more than capable of defending whatever the lack of bounce in the pitch. In all Richards had hit twenty-one fours and five sixes, but it was not so much the mere statistics as the method in which the runs were accumulated that put the innings above many other whirlwind efforts produced in one-day contests.

The many critics of the shortened game claim it needs no science for batsmen, merely the ability to hit long and hard whatever the merits of each ball bowled. Yet Richards applied tactics, especially during the partnership with Holding, which are fundamental to any form of cricket. He farmed the bowling expertly and paced his innings perfectly – taking few risks when the West Indies' position was precarious but then launching out into his full repertoire once the early disasters had been cancelled out. Furthermore, he scored his runs against Botham and Willis, each of whom took in excess of three hundred Test wickets and who deserved respect.

The effect of Richards' century was to knock the stuffing out of the once-confident English team. They lost Graeme Fowler and Mike Gatting with only 8 runs on the board, and while Allan Lamb bounced back to form after a disappointing winter, scoring 75, England were way behind the run rate when they were bowled out for 168 in the fiftieth over, suffering defeat by 104 runs.

Although England came back well to win the second one-day international two days later at Trent Bridge, they lost the third and the one-day series at Lord's and went on to suffer their first ever five–nil whitewash in the Tests that followed. England had begun so confidently at Manchester, but after Richards' intervention there was never quite the same assurance from the home team during the rest of the summer; that one great innings almost certainly fashioned the events that followed.

A one man show – the scorecard reveals Viv Richards' total domination at Old Trafford:

West Indies

C. G. Greenidge	c Bairstow b Botham	9
D. L. Haynes	run out	1
R. B. Richardson	c and b Willis	6
I. V. A. Richards	not out	189
H. A. Gomes	b Miller	4
C. H. Lloyd	c Pringle b Miller	8
P. J. Dujon	c Gatting b Miller	0
M. D. Marshall	run out	4
E. A. E. Baptiste	c Bairstow b Botham	26
J. Garner	c and b Foster	3
M. A. Holding	not out	12
Extras		10
Total	(55 overs)	272–9

Fall of wickets: 5, 11, 43, 63, 89, 98, 102, 161, 166

Bowling:	Willis	11–2–38–1
	Botham	11–0–67–2
	Foster	11–0–61–1
	Miller	11–1–32–3
	Pringle	11–0–64–0

England

C. Fowler	c Lloyd b Garner	1
T. A. Lloyd	c Dujon b Holding	15
M. W. Gatting	lbw Garner	0
D. I. Gower	c Greenidge b Marshall	15
A. J. Lamb	c Richardson b Gomes	75
I. T. Botham	c Richardson b Baptiste	2
D. L. Bairstow	c Garner b Richards	13
G. Miller	b Richards	7
D. R. Pringle	c Garner b Holding	6
N. A. Foster	b Garner	24
R. G. D. Willis	not out	1
Extras		9
Total	(50) overs	168

Fall of wickets: 7, 8, 33, 48, 51, 80, 100, 115, 162

Bowling:	Garner	8.8–0–18–3
	Holding	11–2–23–2
	Baptiste	11–0–38–1
	Marshall	6–1–20–1
	Richards	11–1–45–2
	Gomes	3–0–15–1

West Indies won by 104 runs
Man of the match: I. V. A. Richards

Gordon Greenidge
Lord's, 1984

The summer of 1984 could be looked at in two ways. From an English point of view it consisted of months of deepening depression as one defeat followed another, but for the West Indies it was one long cheerful calypso that reached a climax at The Oval in August when victory by 172 runs completed a five–nil whitewash in the series. The record books had to be rewritten, and while there had been little doubt for several years no further evidence was required to crown Clive Lloyd's team the undisputed kings of world cricket. Yet in retrospect it is easy to forget that on two occasions during the series the West Indies found themselves deep in trouble, and each time they were hauled out of it by the batting of Gordon Greenidge. The opener's painstaking 223 in ten hours during the Old Trafford Test was a masterful display of concentration and controlled aggression, but the innings which clinched victory in the Second Test at Lord's was something very special.

The West Indies had been expected to win the series long before it started, and they arrived in England equipped with their usual battery of fast bowlers and with four world-class batsmen – Greenidge, Lloyd, Viv Richards and Desmond Haynes – all at the peak of their careers. They turned their potential superiority into hard fact in the opening Test at Edgbaston. With Joel Garner taking nine wickets and Larry Gomes scoring a century alongside Richards, to confirm that even their second-string batsmen were no pushovers, the West Indies completed victory inside four days by an innings and 180 runs.

Despite the yawning gap between the two sides and cloudy weather, headquarters was packed as the two teams met for a second time, and English supporters were suddenly given a glimmer of hope. The eye injury suffered by Andy Lloyd in the First Test forced the home selectors to make a change at the top of the order and they arrived at the pairing of Chris Broad and Graeme Fowler, which with skipper David Gower stationed to bat first wicket down meant that the top three were all left-handers.

Although asked to bat first in gloomy conditions that seemed tailor-made for Garner and Malcolm Marshall, Broad and Fowler responded with a century open stand. Broad, upright at the crease, ignored any temptation to dabble outside the off stump and powerfully punished anything on his legs. The much smaller Fowler looked less tidy and was often beaten, but what he lacked in technique he more than compensated for with graft and sheer guts. Although Broad marked his debut with 55 in a shade over two and a half hours, Fowler, despite regularly losing partners, went on to score 106 in 6 hours 6 minutes, and given the severity of the defeat in Birmingham England's total of 286 represented something of a comeback.

By the close of the second day it even began to look impressive as Ian Botham, bowling with the fire that had been more often associated with the early years of his career, fired out the first three West Indian batsmen with only 35 runs scored in reply. Greenidge fell to a slip catch by Geoff Miller, Gomes was superbly taken at short leg by Mike Gatting, and Haynes returned to the famous old pavilion trapped leg before.

It was left to Lloyd and his vice-captain Richards to stabilise the innings, and as Saturday brought with it sunny weather, it appeared that either could crown a glorious day with a century. But Botham, swinging the ball either way, had other ideas as he bowled a cruelly long unchanged spell from the Pavilion End. Lloyd was made to labour for fifty-nine balls, adding only 7 to his overnight 32 before the England all-rounder claimed his second lbw in a match which equalled the previous Test record of twelve such decisions. Among the other victims was Richards, dismissed by a ball which cut back considerably and which led to considerable controversy later in the day when umpire Barrie Meyer admitted publicly that he had apologised to the West Indian because he 'may have made a mistake'. After Richards' 72 only Eldine Baptiste, with a free-flowing 44, stood up to England's attack. Botham picked up five of the seven wickets to fall on the third day to finish with eight for 103, and with the West Indies bowled out for 245 England began their second innings with a 41-run advantage.

At first England failed to cash in as the three left-handers were sent packing before another 36 runs had been added, but two stands gave Gower's men hope. First Allan Lamb and Gatting added 52 for the fourth wicket and they were parted only when the Middlesex man

Gordon Greenidge cuts loose on his way to a double ton at Lord's . . .

was lbw for the second time in the match without offering a stroke to Marshall – another dubious judgement that was to haunt him for years afterwards.

After rain made Monday morning something of a misery, Lamb then enjoyed a partnership of 128 minutes with Ian Botham in which England's batting looked better than at any other time in the summer. As Lamb chugged along towards a well-earned century, Botham hit one six and nine fours on his way to 81 before being struck on the pads by Garner. With a lead of 257 at the fall of the fifth wicket it was touch and go whether England would be dismissed to leave the West Indies with a fairly straightforward target on the last day, or whether Gower would find himself in a rare position of strength to make a declaration. Some thought the England captain would make that move in the final hour of the fourth day, but Lamb and Paul Downton accepted bad light with 53 minutes to go, much to the disgust of the critics, who argued that it was a tactical mistake. In the event England added 13 more runs on the Tuesday morning before Gower declared at 300 for 9, setting a target of 342 to win in five and a half hours.

Since the ball had swung considerably throughout the first four days England had every reason to be confident of making the West Indies struggle, with a good chance of drawing level in the series. But it was not to be. Although Haynes was run out by Lamb after he and Greenidge had put on 57 for the first wicket, it was to be the home side's only breakthrough and the exhilarating play that followed was dominated by Greenidge.

The thirty-three-year-old Barbados-born (but Reading-educated) opener was no stranger to English crowds as he had been breaking bowlers' hearts in the County Championship since 1970 when John Arlott had talked him into joining Hampshire. And successive England selectors had often had cause to regret that as a teenager Greenidge had opted to play for the West Indies when he was eligible for both nations.

Although Greenidge actually began the run chase in a somewhat tentative fashion, he had already made 110 before he offered England the first chance of his wicket – an edge off Willis that flew hard to Botham, by then England's lone fielder in the slips, but went to ground. While Gomes was content to play the quiet, assured foil at one end, and as movement through the air, so regularly evident to all the bowlers on the first four days, declined, Greenidge unleashed his full repertoire of murderous strokes.

. . . and celebrates a remarkable victory with Larry Gomes

Hampshire watchers had long since recognised that when Greenidge began to limp at the crease he could be at his most dangerous, and when in mid afternoon England spotted that his creaking knees were beginning to falter it was an ominous sign. Many of his early boundaries among the twenty-nine fours he hit in total came from savage square-cuts as he made the most of the nearness of the ropes on either side of the wicket. But once Gower finally worked out his field to cut down that supply of runs, Greenidge simply switched to begin peppering mid-wicket and long-on as each English bowler was coldly destroyed in turn.

It says much for the dominance of Greenidge that the West Indies, who had been expected to have to work hard for their victory, completed a nine-wicket win with 11.5 of the final 20 overs to spare and had no need to call upon the powers of quality batsmen such as Lloyd and Richards who spent the afternoon padded up on the pavilion balcony. When the game ended Greenidge had scored an unbeaten 214 – only Don Bradman and Wally Hammond had scored more in a Test at Lord's. Greenidge had completed his first double-century for the West Indies with a top-edged hook for six, and had batted for exactly five hours. With Gomes, by comparison almost sedate in his progress to 92, he had added 287 in only 236 minutes to set a new record for a West Indian second-wicket stand against England.

Gower looked somewhat shell-shocked as he watched Richards collect the winners' cheque from the sponsors. England had certainly been on even terms throughout the first four days, and occasionally on top, yet he had the dubious distinction of becoming the first England captain since Norman Yardley in 1948 to declare in the second innings and lose. Arguments raged for days afterwards over the timing of his declaration, but the bottom line showed that the England skipper had not blundered – his side had simply been flattened by the brilliance of one man.

Malcolm Marshall
Headingley, 1984

Seated in the packed stands at Headingley in 1984, spectators could almost feel the tremendous sense of relief vibrating out of the English dressing room shortly after the start of the Third Test against the West Indies. Two defeats in arrears after as many matches in the five-Test summer series, David Gower's heavily criticised and beleaguered team was well aware that it needed some drastic change of fortune to maintain any chance of halting a Caribbean victory march in its tracks – and with the game barely an hour old, a small chink of light had suddenly appeared at the end of the tunnel.

Malcolm Marshall, feared as the fastest of the four West Indian bowlers employed in the match, had broken his thumb. He had dived in the gully to stop a shot from opening batsman Chris Broad, climbed painfully back on to his feet clutching his left hand and rushed off the field for treatment. The twenty-six-year-old mean machine from Barbados had already served due notice that he was in top form for the Test by delivering 6 lively overs with the new ball at a cost of just 4 runs, but suddenly there were grave doubts over whether he would be able to take any further part in the match. As Broad said later:

> We were struggling in the series and desperately in need of a break or two. When the news reached us that Malcolm might not bowl again in the Test it was not so much a question of sighs of relief in our dressing room – more a genuine celebration. Obviously we had sympathy with any player getting hurt, but we thought that the West Indies, being a bowler short, would not be able to keep up the pressure with the sort of never-ending pace barrage that had beaten us in the past.

England's jubilation, however, was to be short-lived as Marshall, known to his friends as 'Macho', lived up to his rugged nickname with a fearsome second-innings performance that was to swing the match West Indies' way.

Despite the enormous boost to English morale caused by Marshall's early exit on the first morning, the home side still struggled batting first. Headingley served up a cool, overcast day which helped the ball swing, and a pitch of less than even bounce undermined the batsmen's confidence to play shots. And while Marshall's searing pace was absent, the West Indies still possessed two bowlers capable of harnessing the conditions for profit. At the ages of thirty-two and thirty respectively, Joel Garner and Michael Holding had long since learnt that pace was not a vital ingredient when the ball was playing tricks.

England quickly lost Graeme Fowler, Paul Terry and Gower, with Garner trapping the two left-handers leg before wicket, and when spinner Roger Harper, bowling earlier than expected because of Marshall's absence, accounted for Broad they were in trouble at 87 for 4. It was only Allan Lamb and to a lesser extent Ian Botham who prevented a landslide. Botham made 45, while Lamb went on to score exactly 100, his second ton in consecutive Test innings, which made him the first England batsman to achieve the feat against the West Indies since Ken Barrington in 1960.

England's fairly modest total of 270 gained an air of respectability as soon as the visitors began their reply. Paul Allott, of Lancashire, playing his first Test after a two-year absence from the international scene, copied the Garner and Holding technique of line and length to take four early wickets to reduce the West Indies to 239 for 7 by the close of the second day, and the match had developed into a level, if low-scoring contest.

A big Saturday crowd had every reason to hope that England might gain a first-innings advantage, but first the bowlers had to see off Larry Gomes who had already made a ton in the First Test at Birmingham and was on course for a second. At first he was assisted by Holding who damaged England's hopes with a series of furious strokes, particularly against big Bob Willis, hitting five sixes on his way to 59.

When Holding was finally caught by Allott in the deep and Garner was run out soon afterwards, it was widely assumed that the West Indies innings would close at 290 for 9 with Gomes marooned on 96. But to the astonishment of the crowd and disappointment of the English side, Marshall suddenly appeared at the bottom of the pavilion steps. Disregarding the pain in his left hand and scorning the use of a helmet, he was prepared to follow in the brave footsteps of Lionel Tennyson and Colin Cowdrey and bat one-handed in a Test.

Malcolm Marshall attempting a one-handed drive against Paul Allott at Leeds

With his arm heavily covered in bandages Marshall swished away one-handed in the general direction of the ball for 16 minutes, picking up one four to the third-man boundary, while Gomes reached three figures and stretched the West Indies total to 302 for a lead of 32.

Although Marshall eventually fell to a catch by Botham, he then delivered an even greater shock ten minutes later by taking the field with the rest of the West Indian team at the start of the England second innings and promptly pacing out his run to take the new ball. There was a slight delay while the umpires decided he should cover his injury with a skin-coloured dressing instead of white to avoid distracting the batsmen, but once it had been sorted out England's worst fears materialised.

He quickly dealt with Broad, producing a snorting delivery which reared off a length towards the batsman's throat and presented Eldine Baptiste with a straightforward catch. Before England had knocked off the deficit Marshall struck again with a ball of fullish length which moved just enough to pick up Paul Terry lbw. A positive third-wicket stand of 91 between Gower and Fowler took England into the lead, but just when they were getting on top Harper found the top edge of Gower's bat.

That was the signal for Marshall to return to the attack. He had already proved before lunch that his injured hand was not greatly affecting his performance as a bowler, and even limited to the use of one hand he proved he could field as well, using it to pick up a return catch off Fowler, who had made 50. He then added further to England's misery by producing a ball which kept low to account for Lamb – after his two tons the Northants man was brought back to earth with only 3 to his name.

Although the normally belligerent Ian Botham had showed unusual restraint as he batted for over an hour for 14 by the close of Saturday's play, he had fallen to Garner and England were just 103 ahead with five wickets left.

The traditional Sunday rest day gave Marshall more time to come to terms with his injury, and by the time the game resumed on the Monday he was back at his destructive best. With clouds still hanging around, he cut his pace to generate more swing and the result was four more wickets as England's last hope of resistance, Paul Downton, was caught behind, Derek Pringle and Allott were lbw victims and Nick Cook was caught at slip by Clive Lloyd.

A century partnership between Gordon Greenidge and Desmond Haynes allowed the West Indies to knock off the 128 they required for victory with more than a day and eight wickets in hand, to take the series three–nil.

Surprisingly the Man of the Match award went to Gomes for his century rather than to Marshall, who had overcome his handicap to finish with career-best figures of seven for 53 in 26 overs during England's second innings. But maybe it wasn't so surprising for, as Broad remarked, 'I honestly don't think Malcolm thought too much about the injury – he's not a bowler who uses his front arm that much in his action. He was still a good enough bowler, broken thumb or not, to make the most of the conditions at Leeds.' But Marshall was ruled out of any other cricket for almost a fortnight while the thumb healed; many cricketers would have pulled out of the match as soon as the injury occurred, without waiting to see if they could have carried on.

A broken thumb did not prevent him dismissing England's Chris Broad

Sri Lanka *v.* England
Lord's, 1984

The arrival of the Sri Lankans in England in late July 1984 was seen as an opportunity for a touch of welcome light relief for a beleaguered cricketing nation. The home side, under the new leadership of David Gower, was living through the nightmare of its first ever five–nil whitewash at the hands of the West Indies and it was widely expected that the Sri Lankans, elected to Test status just three years earlier and still wet behind the ears in international cricket, would go to Lord's in August for their first ever Test at cricket's headquarters and receive a thrashing.

Sri Lanka had entered the Test arena in 1982, also against England, losing inside four days in Colombo to Keith Fletcher's Indian tourists by seven wickets. Although the traditional Test calendar allowed the islanders few opportunities to sharpen up their skills, they had still played eleven Tests by the time they reached England and had achieved only two draws alongside nine defeats.

They were still, therefore, going through a learning process and the main purpose of their mini-tour to England, according to manager Neil Chanmugam, was to get his exciting crop of stroke-players to learn basic five-day discipline – to punish the bad balls and pay due respect to the good ones rather than throwing the bat at anything that moved. Five days at Lord's, under the closest scrutiny of the experts, were to prove they were good learners, and the cheerful, almost cheeky way they humbled the country that had invented the game was to win the Sri Lankans many new friends.

The origins of England's poor showing in the match can be traced back to the weekend prior to its start when the home selectors broke from tradition and named exactly eleven players, rather than the normal twelve, to face the Sri Lankans, including only one spinner – the Surrey veteran Pat Pocock – which limited the options open to Gower. The failing was compounded on the opening morning when, with Lord's bathed in a hazy sunshine, Gower hoped the ball would swing to justify the inclusion of four pacemen and chose to bowl first. In the event it was to be the mild pace of the pitch rather than the overhead conditions which proved most influential and England

The Sri Lankan heroes at Lord's: Amal Silva . . .

would have been better served batting first and gaining the upper hand against a Sri Lankan attack that contained only three front-line bowlers.

By close of play on the first day the underdogs had reached 226 for 3, due mainly to the calmness of their opener Sidath Wettimuny who refused to be unnerved by the early loss of Amal Silva and Ranjan Madugalle and began to establish control in a 101-run third-wicket stand with Roy Dias. Despite an attack of cramp, Wettimuny, displaying the straightest of defences but loath not to attack anything loose, contributed 116 in the first six hours of the match. He was to bat through the second day as well, but was forced to live in the shadow of his captain, Duleep Mendis.

After Arjuna Ranatunga, a twenty-one-year-old full of promise, had made a dashing 84, Mendis set out to destroy England's arrogance. Ian Botham thought he had the measure of the stocky little Sri Lankan, working on the theory that he might be vulnerable to the short delivery. Botham set two men back on the leg side for the hook, dropped the ball in short three times in 2 overs, and could only stand and watch in frustration as Mendis stroked him wristily over the boundary for six. Lord's gave Mendis a standing ovation when he reached his hundred off only 112 deliveries, and a similar reception awaited Wettimuny when finally on Saturday morning he edged Paul Allott into the gloves of wicket-keeper Paul Downton.

Batting for 10 hours and 42 minutes for 190 Wettimuny had played the longest Test innings ever seen at Lord's, had made the highest score by a batsman on his first Test appearance in England, and only six other visiting batsmen, including the mighty Don Bradman and Gordon Greenidge, had ever scored more at HQ. Furthermore, throughout his stay at the crease he never offered a single chance as Leicestershire's Jon Agnew, playing in only his second Test and looking for an easier life having made his debut against the West Indies, explained:

> Wettimuny's innings was the best I have ever seen. As it wore on I began to think we would never get him out. There was a short boundary on the Tavern side and anything wide of him was despatched there immediately. He was immensely strong off the back foot and just stood there waiting for the right ball to hit – he didn't take any risks and I don't think he offered a chance.

. . . Duleep Mendis . . .

With only three bowlers up his sleeve it was somewhat surprising when Mendis decided to declare at 491 for 7 instead of putting more pressure on England's batsmen by giving them a target well in excess of 300 just to save the follow-on, but given his side's domination of the first two days it quickly transpired that he had not miscalculated. After Graeme Fowler had departed cheaply Chris Tavaré and Chris Broad went into their shells, reducing Saturday afternoon at Lord's – normally the highlight of any English cricket summer – to a crawl as they scored only 49 runs in 27 overs. Gower was forced to admit at a press conference later that day: 'That kind of cricket is no fun to watch and it is certainly worse to play like it.' The two England batsmen were to pay dearly for the ridicule heaped on England that day as Broad, who had fought so bravely against the West Indians, found himself out in the cold a fortnight later when the winter tour party was picked for India, while Tavaré was not to earn an England recall until 1989 when England found themselves in trouble against the Australians.

Gower himself was hardly more assertive, making 16 on the third day and needing two more hours on the Bank Holiday Monday to reach 55 as many in a 7000 crowd felt they would have done better to stay at home and mow the lawn. England would have been in total disarray had it not been for Allan Lamb, who followed up his fighting three centuries against the West Indies with 107, but at 370 all out England still conceded a first-innings lead of 120.

Arguments raged afterwards as to whether Gower should have opened up the game by declaring soon after the follow-on was averted, throwing down a challenge to Mendis to set England a target on the final day, but with a moral victory already in the bag it was doubtful whether the Sri Lankan skipper would have responded. Instead he allowed his young batsmen to gain further Test experience, with Silva making 102. In his own second innings, packed full of more glorious shots, Mendis went to within 6 runs of becoming only the second batsman in history, after West Indian George Headley in 1939, to score two centuries in a Test at Lord's.

Sri Lanka's performance in their first Test in England earned them a mention in every BBC World Service news bulletin for almost a complete week and marked the nation's emergence at international level. Within thirteen months their players had matured sufficiently to record their first Test victory when they beat India by 149 runs at the Saravanamuttu Stadium, Colombo, in September 1985.

. . . *Siddath Wettimuny*

Allan Border
Trinidad, 1984

The staging of the Nehru Cup in October 1989 held little significance for the cricketing world in general – it was just another in a long series of one-day jamborees designed to boost the depleted coffers of yet another cricket authority unable to support the game on the dwindling receipts from Test matches. To the host nation, India, it had added significance since it celebrated the centenary of the founding of a political dynasty and was aimed at bolstering support for the ailing government of Prime Minister Rajiv Ghandi. In a country where cricket is almost a religion, it must have been more than small coincidence that match attendances were in general poor, India failed to reach the final and within a month of the trophy being handed to bitter rivals Pakistan, Mr Ghandi lost a general election.

There were less than a handful of memorable performances during the Nehru Cup, though one in particular stands out because it was totally out of character for the player involved. For almost all of the eleven years Allan Border had spent playing Test cricket, his batting had been fighting a lost cause, and it was almost unavoidable that the typical Border innings would be described as gutsy, dependable and defensive, unlike the majestic adjectives conferred on contemporaries such as Viv Richards and David Gower, yet his Test record eclipsed them both.

At Hyderabad in the Nehru Cup, however, a crowd of barely 15,000 saw a new side of Border as he butchered England's attack with an innings of 84 from forty-four balls, his five sixes including three off successive balls from Gladstone Small and a remarkably improvised drive against Derek Pringle which planted a low full toss way over the ropes at deep extra cover. Border himself admitted after the game: 'I don't think I have ever hit the ball so hard over such a long period before. I've tried often enough, but it's just gone straight up in the air.' But perhaps the most telling comment on the day came from Alan Crompton, the Australian team manager, who added: 'When you have seen an innings like that from Allan it makes you wonder just what might have happened had many of his Test-match innings been played under different circumstances. He has achieved so much in his career yet so often his game has been dictated by the position of his team. Who knows what he might have achieved had he been allowed to play with more freedom?'

In terms of cricketing satisfaction nothing pleased Border more than leading Australia to their four–nil victory over England in the 1989 Ashes series after having been involved in three previous attempts to win on the oldest enemy's territory that had ended in failure. But of the twenty-two Test centuries he had scored leading up to that triumph, none had given him more pleasure than his performance in the Second Test against the West Indies at Port of Spain, Trinidad, in March 1984. Border commented: 'Critics have said it was my finest hour in cricket. I prefer to regard it as my finest ten hours.' In fact, his two innings in the match were the best examples of the role he had so often been forced to play.

The Australian side which visited the Caribbean that spring had reached a watershed. Just prior to the tour beginning, legends from the previous decade had bowed out through retirement, robbing skipper Kim Hughes of the services of Greg Chappell, Dennis Lillee and Rod Marsh. Furthermore Graham Yallop, who had been the side's leading run-scorer in the recently ended series against Pakistan, had been forced to remain at home with a knee injury. And Hughes knew he faced a daunting task against a West Indies side which he described as 'the strongest, most professional and most disciplined' he had ever seen.

Despite Hughes' gloomy predictions, the First Test ended in a draw. Rain washed out all but 71 minutes of the first day's play at Georgetown, Guyana, but Australia picked up a useful first-innings lead of 49 and Hughes even had the luxury of a second-innings declaration to set the West Indies a target of 323 to win in 260 minutes. The run chase proved too stiff, but a record West Indian opening partnership of 250 between Gordon Greenidge and Desmond Hayes warned the Aussies that they would have to struggle to bowl the opposition out twice to win a Test.

The Australians were offered some respite when West Indian skipper Clive Lloyd pulled out of the Second Test with hamstring trouble, but his stand-in Viv Richards quickly spotted the possibilities in a green and damp pitch. He left out off-spinner Roger Harper to make room for an extra pace bowler in Milton Small, and when he won the toss he had no hesitation in asking the opposition to bat first. On a lively surface the tall Joel Garner was almost unplayable – his fourth ball reared to have Keppler Wessels caught at fourth slip, in his second over Greg Ritchie moved across his stumps and was bowled, and Wayne Phillips could only turn another fiery lifting delivery into the hands of wicket-keeper Jeff Dujon. By the time rain brought a premature halt to the first day Hughes had also edged Garner behind and the Australians were happy to dive for cover at 55 for 4, with Garner having claimed all four wickets at a cost of 22 runs in 8 destructive overs.

If the Australians were going to fight back on the second day they had to rely on Border and the experience of David Hookes, and the South Australian left-hander briefly threatened with 23 before falling to a Garner yorker. Thus Border found himself in an all too familiar position, but he was able to coax a 103-run partnership out of the young Dean Jones, and a further 49 was put on with Geoff Lawson.

After rain had again called an early end to the second day, the third morning developed into two separate battles. At one end Wayne Daniel worked his way steadily through the Australian tail, while at the other Border was having his own contest with a bowler more than a foot taller than himself. Garner continually banged the ball in short and Border, rising to the tip of his toes, fended it off gamely as he approached a much-deserved century. Garner eventually kept Border scoreless for 27 minutes and twelve deliveries as the scoreboard tantalisingly showed 98 beside his name, and the West Indian then cruelly bowled Alderman to leave him stranded. By batting through from an uncertain start with relentless determination, Border had ensured that the Australian total would look respectable at 255 all out.

A lot of the moisture had worked its way out of the track by the time the West Indies began their first innings, and by the end of the third day they had moved to within 37 of the Australian total. Desmond Haynes and Viv Richards each made half-centuries, but they were merely a prelude to a thunderous sixth-wicket stand of 158 on the fourth day between Gus Logie and Dujon which took the West Indies towards a huge lead. Logie made 97, Dujon 130 – his second Test century – and when Garner added to his six-wicket haul by weighing in with 24, Richards was able to declare at 468 for 8 shortly after tea.

Grim determination – Allan Border's hallmark

The West Indies' lead of 213 began to take on unmanageable proportions as the Australians lost Phillips, run out with only 1 on the board, and by the close of the fourth day he had been joined in the pavilion by Wessels and Ritchie. Australia's chances of survival rested with Border, who recalled 'I had made up my mind that if I was going to join the procession back to the pavilion it was going to be after a fight.'

Throughout the fifth morning Border stood up to a succession of short deliveries and at times found partners willing to hang around with him, but just as quickly as stands began to develop they were destroyed. Hughes made 33 before Marshall trapped him leg before, Hookes made 21 but then fell to the part-time bowling of Richie Richardson, and Jones could not recapture his first-innings form, scoring only 5 before he was bowled by Richards. Tom Hogan lent valuable support, scoring 38, but when Australia's number nine Rodney Hogg arrived at the crease at 196 for 8, his team were still 17 runs short of avoiding an innings defeat and there were still three hours of the match to be played out. 'We were in a position comparable to Custer and his Seventh Cavalry at Little Big Horn,' wrote Border later.

Hogg, not highly regarded in Test batting circles, hung around with Border for an hour, taking the score to 238 and at least making sure the West Indies would have to bat again, but when he became Richards' second victim defeat was still written on the wall.

But Hogg had obviously inspired Alderman to produce an innings way above his normal station. Running sharply between the wickets to give Border as much of the strike as possible, he kept the left-hander company until well inside the final 20 overs. Border played on tenterhooks. He knew that mere survival at the crease would not be enough on its own to save the game, for if the final wicket went at the other end the West Indies would be left with a simple run dash to the finishing line. He had to keep the score ticking along as well, and he did it to great effect. While Alderman made 21, Border approached the century that had eluded him in the first innings. During the last half-hour Richards could have accepted the draw at any time, but in a sporting gesture to recognise Border's rearguard action he kept his team on the pitch until the Australian produced a straight-driven four to reach three figures with 3.5 of the final 20 overs remaining. Border had taken the Australians from the desolation of 41 for 3 to eventual safety at 299 for 9, and the West Indies appreciated the efforts of the underdog. Border recalled:

> Viv paid me the compliment of allowing me to complete the century before he acknowledged a draw – a very sporting gesture. The crowd also turned it on for us. It was standing ovation stuff. Hoggy, Terry and I had seen out 160 minutes of sheer pressure to save a game which was by all logic and things reasonable lost. Terry had been with me for the last 105 minutes. I reckon he deserved heaps of credit but the strength of the crowd's reception surprised me. West Indian fans are fiercely parochial and regard the other team, whoever they are, as villains, the enemy. Yet they were treating us like home-town heroes.

Border paid fair dues to Alderman, but in a match where no other Australian could manage a half-century he had himself batted for ten and a half hours, faced 535 mainly hostile deliveries and repulsed everything from the opposition. Under enormous pressure Border scored 198 runs in two innings without being dismissed – what would he have been capable of in a strident winning side?

Richard Ellison
The Oval, 1985

One dominant theme ran through each of the first four Tests in the 1985 Ashes series in England. Although the two teams assembled in mid August at Edgbaston for the Fifth with the honours even at one victory apiece, neither England nor Australia had unearthed a pace bowler, or combination of pace bowlers, that looked capable of turning the contest decisively in one direction.

Although England captain David Gower possessed in his armoury the talents of Ian Botham, he was not generally thought to be the same powerful force that had turned the previous Ashes encounter in Birmingham four years earlier with a spell of five wickets for 1 run in twenty-eight balls. The selectors had also at various times given him Norman Cowans, Paul Allott, Arnie Sidebottom, Neil Foster and Jon Agnew without achieving the desired effect.

The Australians were having similar problems. With his thirty-fifth birthday falling in mid season, Jeff Thomson was but a shade of the terrorising fast bowler who had formed such a devastating partnership with Dennis Lillee in the 1970s; Geoff Lawson, a success in England in 1981, was plagued by bronchial troubles; while youngsters Simon O'Donnell and Dave Gilbert were still learning the art. Their one consolation was the emergence of twenty-year-old Craig McDermott, a red-headed tearaway from Queensland who captured eight wickets for 141 in England's only innings in the rain-hit Fourth Test at Old Trafford, but whose young shoulders were too raw to carry the complete burden of Australian hopes.

The net result of the impotency on both sides was clearly reflected in the batting averages as they squared up in Birmingham. The Australians had already accumulated a total of five Test centuries in the summer, including a match-winning 196 from skipper Allan Border at Lord's and 172 from Graeme Wood in the drawn game at Trent Bridge. England's three hundreds included the 175 from Tim Robinson that was largely responsible for the victory in the opening encounter at Leeds, and 166 from Gower at Nottingham.

With the distinct advantage of being able to scour all seventeen first-class counties for talent at a time of scarcity, the England selectors came up with their fifth different permutation of fast bowlers for Edgbaston, with Botham the only survivor from the opening game. With Agnew being made twelfth man it meant a long-awaited debut for Leicestershire's Les Taylor and the recall of Kent's Richard Ellison.

Taylor, a lingering reminder of the days when counties shouted down the coal mines to find new fast-bowling talent (he had worked the face at Bagworth colliery in his younger days), might have played for England earlier had he not been given a three-year Test ban for his part in the 1982 unofficial tour to South Africa. Tall and broad-shouldered, he often generated more pace than was apparent to those seated on the boundary edge, and with a chest-on action he generally moved the ball into the right-hander with the aid of the seam.

Ellison's background could not have been more different. His family was steeped in cricketing tradition, his great-grandfather having played against the Grace brothers in the nineteenth century and his grandfather having captained Derbyshire Second XI at the age of sixty. Educated at Friars Prep School at Ashford where his stepfather was headmaster, he had moved on to Tonbridge School where he played alongside Chris Cowdrey who was later to become his county captain. Ellison had made his Test debut the previous summer, and five wickets for a losing side in the Fifth Test against the West Indies at The Oval had earned him a winter tour place in India. In three Tests on the sub-continent Ellison was hardly a resounding success, with his four wickets costing 72.75 runs each, but the figures were illusory since he bowled the out-swinger, his stock ball, consistently well, particularly during England's victory at Delhi, without achieving the success he deserved.

In fact the selectors would have turned to his talents long before the fifth month of the season had he not suffered the misfortune of sprained ankle ligaments when he slipped in a wet foothold in April and was forced on to the sidelines for eight weeks. During the two months of inactivity Ellison shed 18lb in weight, mainly by cutting down on his two favourite hobbies – eating and drinking beer – and the selectors had seen enough to call him up for the Fourth Test, but only to make him twelfth man. Indeed, he almost did not play in the Fifth since he arrived at Edgbaston suffering from a cold and England's physiotherapist Bernie Thomas advised against his inclusion.

Richard Ellison swung the 1985 Ashes series England's way

Despite the England team surgery, events on the first day suggested that little had happened to change the general pattern of the series. Although in its recent past Edgbaston had normally provided good, flat batting surfaces, there was sufficient cloud cover and moisture in the pitch for Gower to gamble after winning the toss on asking the Australians to bat. Initially it was not an unwise move as Botham accounted for Wood with the aid of a Phil Edmonds catch, and the Middlesex spinner then confirmed the belief that the pitch possessed more than the odd gremlin by dismissing Aussie vice-captain Andrew Hilditch shortly before lunch with a ball that turned appreciably.

That England made little further progress on the first day was due to two distinct factors: first that there was no play between lunch and 5 p.m. due to rain, and second, their own fielding lapses. As Border and his fellow left-hander Keppler Wessels took the Aussies through to 181 for 2 at stumps, they enjoyed four escapes. Wessels was dropped at slip by Botham, in the covers by Robinson off Ellison, and then by Taylor from his own bowling. Border, with only 1 to his name, could have departed before the first meal break, but Paul Downton missed a tricky stumping off Edmonds.

It was in the two hours before lunch on the Friday at Edgbaston that an Ashes series which had looked so evenly matched was turned on its head by the first bowler to emerge from the pack on either side. Ellison, relishing the continued cloud cover and gentle breeze, bowled a forty-three-ball spell that produced four wickets at a cost of only 12 runs, which was to spook the Australians for the rest of the summer.

The departure of Border began the slide as he attempted to clip an in-swinging delivery through mid-wicket and was well caught down by his ankles by Edmonds, fielding at shortleg. Wessels, having batted obdurately for 228 minutes for 83, was tempted by a ball which left him outside the off stump and was caught behind; Greg Ritchie followed an out-swinger into the hands of Botham at second slip; and when Wayne Phillips attempted to blast the Australians out of trouble, Tim Robinson stooped in the covers to hold on to a stinging catch. Remarkably Ellison had accounted for three top-class left-handers, when it was widely considered that he had difficulty moving the ball away from them as effectively as he did with right-handers. Since Taylor had also nipped in to claim O'Donnell as his first Test victim, the visitors had watched in horror while the scoreboard dived from 189 for 2 to 218 for 7. Between showers in the afternoon, as Ellison tired and Botham proved rather too expensive, the Australian tail fought back led by Lawson, who struck a defiant 53. But with Ellison returning early on the third morning to pick up two more wickets to finish with six for 77, the Australians were bowled out for 335 – hardly a secure total and much less than it would have been without his intervention.

Dawn on Saturday brought with it a welcome change in the weather, clouds giving way to steamy sunshine, and as the Birmingham wicket flattened out England's batsmen, after the early exit of Gooch, ploughed into the Australian attack. As they built a second-wicket stand of 331 – the sixth highest for England in history and the second highest against the Aussies – Gower and Robinson ensured a lead of 20 runs with nine wickets in hand by the close of the third day. Robinson made 148 before he was bowled by Lawson early on the fourth morning, Gower 215 (his second Test double-hundred and only the sixth by an Englishman against Australia), and there

The prize scalp of Aussie skipper Allan Border and Ellison celebrates with Paul Downton

were two cameo innings to follow. Mike Gatting struck an entertaining century, while Botham scored 18 off just eleven balls, the first and third of which produced mighty drives for six off McDermott. But while England played with amazing freedom to reach 595 for 5 declared, a lead of 260, the Australians had still not come to terms with Ellison.

Gower's declaration, which coincided with Gatting reaching three figures, left Border's team with 90 minutes' batting at the end of the fourth day. They responded to the challenge of trying to save the match by collapsing to 37 for 5, Ellison claiming another four wickets in a fourteen-ball spell in the final half-hour. It was the safe hands of the Kent man that began the rout as Hilditch, who was proving to be a reckless hooker, swallowed the bait proffered by Botham and was caught by Ellison, one of two men posted deep on the long-leg boundary. The slump from 32 for 1 was astonishing as Ellison again tempted Wessels outside the off stump, night-watchman Bob Holland played across his first delivery and was lbw, Wood skied a catch to mid-wicket and Border, the one player who might have stood between England and victory, was bowled off his pads.

The weather on the fifth day threatened to take the edge off England's performance as Gower's frustrated team was forced by drizzle to remain in the dressing room until half past two and only two balls were possible before they were again compelled to seek shelter. When the elements finally relented there were 2 hours and 20 minutes of the game remaining, and Ritchie and Phillips were determined to see it through. In a match that had been dominated by superb individual efforts it was a split second of controversy that finally settled the issue. Having struck eleven fluent fours on his way to 53, Phillips was attempting to make it a round dozen when he cut fiercely at Edmonds. The ball ricocheted off the boot of Allan Lamb standing close in at silly point to Gower, who took the catch standing two yards away at short mid-off. As England claimed the catch, Phillips stood his ground until ordered off by umpires David Shepherd and David Constant. Border later claimed that Shepherd could not have seen whether the ball had bounced before striking Lamb and that the evidence from numerous TV replays was inconclusive. The decision, however, finished off the Australians' resistance and they were finally dismissed in the sixth over of the last hour when Botham had McDermott caught close in by Edmonds.

As England's fans celebrated a victory by an innings and 118 runs, Man of the Match adjudicator Fred Trueman had an enormous task. Gower's 215 and his skilled handling of the bowlers deserved recognition, but as a bowler himself he opted instead for Ellison who had finished with match figures of ten for 104.

It was a shrewd judgement, since in Ellison England had at last found a bowler capable of turning the tide. When the two teams met nine days later for the Sixth Test at the Oval, Gower was again in majestic form, scoring 157 to set up another England victory by an innings and 94 runs to complete a three–one victory in the series and win back the Ashes, lost overseas in the winter of 1982–83. Significantly, however, Ellison also played a key role, taking seven more wickets, including five in the Australian second innings, to finish with seventeen in two Tests at an average of 10.88. In three out of four innings he had accounted for Border, who had proved through the summer to be a thorn in England's flesh, and it was only the appearance of Ellison that finally broke his and Australia's resistance.

Richard Hadlee
Brisbane, 1985

The Australians had every reason to respect the strength of the New Zealand tour party which made the short flight across the Tasman Sea to play a three-Test series at the start of November 1985. For almost a decade a Test side of some merit had been emerging, based around the experience of John Wright and Richard Hadlee and the precocious batting talent of Martin Crowe, and the Australians were in no condition to guarantee them a hostile reception. They had just returned from an Ashes series in England where they had been badly mauled by David Gower, and their ranks had been seriously depleted by desertions to a rebel South African tour.

Allan Border's men could at least look to the record books for a shred of comfort, for they revealed that the Kiwis had never previously won a Test in Australia. But all that was soon to change.

Even though he had reached the age of thirty-four, Hadlee, dark-haired, lean and menacing, was to be the crucial figure. While the raw pace and fire of his early youth had long since burned out, Hadlee, as he approached the landmark of 300 wickets in Tests, was a proven match-winner. And he really needed to be at his best in this series, since the support bowlers in the New Zealand side were hardly world class. Martin Snedden was young and brisk but often wayward, Ewen Chatfield economical but barely more than military medium pace, and skipper Jeremy Coney had earned the nickname 'Falling Leaves' since his gentle seamers were so slow they seemed to flutter in the air.

Brisbane was overcast and steamy when Coney won the toss and asked the Australians to bat first on a green wicket, and initially it appeared a justified decision. Aussie opener Andrew Hilditch waited only five balls before attempting his favourite hook shot against Hadlee, but succeeded only in finding the safe hands of Chatfield on the long-leg boundary.

After Keppler Wessels and David Boon had launched an Aussie recovery with a second-wicket stand worth 69 in the morning session, Hadlee gained two vital breakthroughs. Two overs before the lunch break he had Boon caught by Coney at slip for 31, and then with his first ball after the break he accounted for Allan Border. The Australian skipper had warmed up for the Test with a century for Queensland against the tourists earlier in the week, but he had failed to get his new innings under way when he chased a wide delivery and was caught head high by Bruce Edgar in the covers. Although rain interrupted play during the final two sessions of the day, Hadlee had used the time available to have Greg Ritchie superbly held in the slips by Crowe, and the game was interestingly poised at stumps with the Australians 146 for 4. Border was later to write:

> We were anticipating a 'safe total' somewhere in the 300s. Hadlee had taken all four wickets to that stage and obviously he was going to be the danger. Dangerous? He was devastating as he whipped through our middle and lower order. It's fair to say that conditions were ideal for him [overcast and humid] on the first day and there was still a little juice in the wicket when play resumed. But Hadlee used the conditions perfectly. It was a great display of intelligent pace bowling.

It took Hadlee only 5 overs on the second morning to account for Wessels, who had defended dourly for 70. The former South African offered no stroke to the Kiwi's in-swinger and fell lbw to precipitate a collapse that would become part of a new entry in the record books.

While only a further 29 runs were added, Hadlee, supported by some brilliant reflex close catching and bowling with venom to get the maximum out of the pitch, hit the stumps of Wayne Phillips and Greg Matthews and had Craig McDermott and Bob Holland caught near to the wicket. He would have become only the second man in Test history behind Jim Laker to take all ten wickets, but for one interruption. Geoff Lawson, the eighth Australian batsman to be dismissed, attacked spinner Vaughan Brown and looped a catch to mid-wicket. Even if he wasn't the bowler, Hadlee could at least claim a part in the demise of Lawson by calmly accepting the catch.

Hadlee's final analysis of nine for 52 from 23.4 overs was found to be the fourth best bowling performance in Test history. It was eclipsed only by Laker's two bowling performances at Old Trafford in 1956 when he took nineteen wickets against the Australians, and by George Lohman's nine for 28 against South Africa in 1895.

If Hadlee revelled under the Brisbane conditions, then it served only to highlight the weaknesses in the Australian attack. It was pulled apart during a record third-wicket stand of 224 compiled by

Crowe and John Reid at the end of the second day and for much of the third. Crowe made 188, equalling his highest score in Test cricket, and Reid 108, but it was a whirlwind batting performance from Hadlee that proved crucial to the timing of the visitors' declaration at 553 for 7. Hadlee scorched four sixes and four fours in his 54 and it allowed Coney to give his bowlers the luxury of two days in which to dismiss the Australians for a second time.

Australia began on the fourth day 374 in arrears and with barely the slightest chance of survival, and even that disappeared quickly. Chatfield found Wessels' bat and pad and Brown held on to a catch at short leg; Boon edged a catch behind off the same bowler and, unbelievably, Hilditch again fell hooking. It was a shot which had ruined his tour to England, and on this occasion it proved too much for the Australian selectors and he was never again picked for a Test match. By lunch the Australians were 67 for 5.

The home side emerged from the match with some credit only when Border and Matthews launched a valiant fight-back with a stand of 199 which at least ensured that the game would continue into the final day. But shortly before stumps on the fourth, New Zealand took the new ball and once Hadlee had Matthews caught at slip for 115, the end was not far away.

Although Border battled with true grit to finish with 152 not out from seven and a half hours of defiance, there were no more heroes to be found among the Australian tail. The game ended shortly before lunch when Hadlee bowled Holland, claiming his fifteenth victim in a game where his 51.4 overs had cost just 123 runs, and New Zealand cracked the champagne corks after opening the series with victory by an innings and 41 runs.

Despite the drubbing which forced the Australians to make five changes for the Second Test at Sydney and produced another seven wickets for Hadlee, Border's team picked itself up off the floor to level the series with a four-wicket victory. Border certainly thought the tide had turned in his favour. He said later:

> For a while, particularly when we won the Second Test, I thought we had really come to terms with him and I made the mistake of saying so publicly. I should have kept my mouth shut. Like Dennis Lillee and good wine, Hadlee had improved with age. He had lost a little pace but that had made him a more thinking bowler, a more dangerous bowler. We found out about that.

*The telling moment for any batsman as Richard Hadlee approaches
the point of delivery*

I really should have been more prudent. Hadlee is a magnificent bowler and the last thing you do with a bloke like that is shove a psychological weapon into his hands. My comments did just that. They fired him up and gave him a point to prove. Hadlee publicly responded to my opinion by predicting that he'd take twelve wickets in the match. He was wrong. He took eleven.

In fact, the wicket at the WACA in Perth for the third and deciding game in the series should not have benefited Hadlee more than anyone else. As part of a much-needed upgrading of facilities at the ground the square had been recently relaid and it was sluggish – quite unlike the normal conditions prevailing in Western Australia and barely suitable for a Test – but that did not prevent Hadlee proving his point.

Although it was Chatfield who made the early breakthrough when the Australians batted first, Hadlee took five for 65 as they were limited to 203. In response, with Wright and Crowe both scoring seventies, the Kiwis built up a lead of 96. And Hadlee quickly reinforced their position by bowling Robbie Kerr with the fourth ball of the Australian second innings. Boon and, once more, Border fought back on the fourth day in a partnership of 81, but Hadlee hit back and when the Australians were bowled out for 259, New Zealand were left on the final day of the series to score 164 for victory, a task that was achieved with only four wickets falling.

The win gave New Zealand their first ever Test series triumph over the Australians, and it was richly deserved. Although most of it was due to teamwork, team spirit and the skilful leadership of Coney, in Hadlee they undoubtedly possessed the only bowler capable of dominating and thus winning the series. In the three Tests he had taken thirty-three wickets – fourteen more than the six other bowlers used by his side put together – at a cost of only 12.15 runs per victim.

His efforts were best summed up by Henry Blofeld after the opening victory at Brisbane when he wrote: 'Off a 12 pace run he generated more pace than Lawson and McDermott were later able to do off twice that distance. His control was extraordinary, he scarcely wasted a single ball and it did not seem possible that he could beat the bat so often without finding the edge. Hadlee, at the age of 34, was magnificent.'

Graham Gooch
Trinidad, 1986

To beat the West Indies on their home territory in any sort of cricket is one thing, but to upstage Viv Richards when the Master Blaster is in full flow is quite another. But that is exactly what Graham Gooch managed to achieve in 1986.

England's winter tour to the Caribbean had already developed into a steady, disappointing procession of defeats when the two sides met at Trinidad to play the second of four one-day internationals. And a packed crowd at the pretty Port of Spain Oval, with its backdrop of tree-covered hills, was fully justified in expecting another convincing performance from their home heroes.

Although the match had been reduced by early-morning rain to 37 overs, which gave the team batting second a distinct advantage, an upset did not look on the cards as Desmond Haynes and Richie

Graham Gooch showed scant regard for all the West Indian pacemen in Trinidad

Richardson added 69 for the West Indies' second wicket to give their innings a sound base. And it looked even more unlikely when Richards decided it was time to turn nasty against his Somerset team-mate Ian Botham. Together with Richardson the West Indies captain added 117 for the third wicket in only 9 overs, which should have put the game way out of England's reach. From only thirty-nine balls Richards crashed an amazing 82, beginning with a four off Botham which rattled the advertising boards at mid-wicket and ending with a last-over assault against the England all-rounder which included three breathtaking sixes and cost 23 runs.

Tour captain David Gower gave Botham an immediate chance to make amends, sending him out to open the batting alongside Gooch to try to give England a flying start in their pursuit of 230 – or 6.2 runs an over – for victory. The gamble failed, as Botham had made only 8 when he fell to a juggled catch by Richards, but at least England began to consolidate in an 89-run stand between Gooch and Wilf Slack.

Although in steady succession Gooch lost the company of David Gower, Allan Lamb and Peter Willey, the opener gradually increased his own tempo in a one-man victory dash. Lanky Courtney Walsh was driven for a straight six, and even the much-feared Malcolm Marshall was forced to operate with a man on the long-off boundary as Gooch flayed the bowling all over the Park. Even so, 50 runs were still wanted off the last five overs – a stiff task against bowling of the highest quality – but Gooch was up to it as he moved past the hundred mark, and eventually 9 were wanted off the last over.

The first two balls from Patrick Patterson produced singles, and Gooch pulled the third to mid-wicket for four. Gooch gained another single off the fourth and then ran a cheeky bye to the wicket-keeper as his partner David Smith failed to connect the off stump. Although the final ball of the game rapped him on the pads, Gooch scampered a single which just beat a throw to the bowler's end to complete a stunning English victory by five wickets – their first ever in a limited-overs international in the West Indies.

In his match-winning innings of 129 Gooch hit seventeen fours as well as the six off Walsh and provided the ideal answer to at least one small group of West Indians. Protesters had hung an effigy of the England batsman from a lamp-post outside the ground, complaining about his links with South Africa. But in the end more than 10,000 of their countrymen stood to applaud a magnificent performance.

Even the locals appreciated his ton

John Bracewell
Trent Bridge, 1986

It took forty-eight years and exactly the same number of Test matches before New Zealand finally broke the ice at Wellington in 1978 and recorded their first victory over England. Five years later they went one stage further and won on English soil at Leeds by five wickets, though defeats in the same series at The Oval and Lord's ensured that they returned home from the four-match series empty-handed. However, as the least populated of the world's cricketing nations had grown progressively stronger under the successive captaincies of Geoff Howarth and Jeremy Coney, it appeared only a matter of time before the Kiwis would win a series in England for the first time, especially since England had lost one–nil in New Zealand under the captaincy of Bob Willis early in 1984.

If ever the time was ripe for New Zealand to break their duck in England, it was in the second half of the summer of 1986. The home side approached the series with fortunes at a low ebb. England had begun the year in the Caribbean and had suffered their second successive whitewash at the hands of the West Indies. In a summer season split into two three-match series they had slipped even further, losing two–nil to India and parting company with captain David Gower along the way. By the time the series against New Zealand began they were also without the services of Ian Botham, who was under suspension after admitting in a national newspaper that he had smoked cannabis – a story which had its origins in the 1984 clash between the two sides.

If England's approach to the series was in something of a crisis, then New Zealand's, while certainly more controlled, was nevertheless highly unconventional. It had been agreed with Lord's that Richard Hadlee, their main potential match-winner, would play only in the Tests while spending the rest of his time with Nottinghamshire, by whom he had been granted a benefit. On the administrative side their tour plans were forced to change when manager Bob Vance had to return home early through illness. In his place emerged a triumvirate headed by coach Glenn Turner, assisted by bowler Ewen Chatfield during long periods when he was sidelined by injury, and opening batsman Bruce Edgar, a qualified accountant, who acted as team treasurer.

There was a great deal of logic in New Zealand's handling of Hadlee. Among the members of the tour party were the three young fast bowlers Derek Stirling, Willie Watson and Brian Barrett, all of whom were given greater opportunities by Hadlee's absence to gain useful experience in normally meaningless warm-up matches against the counties. The thirty-five-year-old Hadlee, on the other hand, maintained his cutting edge playing in the County Championship.

The Kiwis also showed a strange attitude to convention in the First Test at Lord's by agreeing to an outrageous use of substitutes by England. The home side could have been struggling when, on the second day, their wicket-keeper Bruce French turned his head into a Hadlee bouncer and left the field groggy and with a cut that was to require three stitches. Although the England XI already contained Bill Athey, a batsman who had been used by both Yorkshire and Gloucestershire in the past as an emergency keeper, the New Zealand management agreed to a series of English alternatives. First Bob Taylor, whose fifty-seven Test-match career had ended in retirement two years earlier, was allowed to don the gloves after being summoned from a Lord's lunch tent where he was entertaining guests on behalf of the match sponsors Cornhill. Then twenty-four hours later, when Taylor, at the age of forty-five, complained of stiffness, they agreed to England using Bobby Parks, the Hampshire wicket-keeper, who was called out of his bed early on Saturday.

If, when French felt well enough to resume his duties on the Monday, England's fans and players felt justified in thinking there was something soft about the 1986 New Zealand side, it was an illusion that was to be quickly dispelled. For it was only a brilliant second-innings 183 from Graham Gooch and the loss of much of the fourth day's play that prevented the tourists from forcing a winning position in the opening Test.

From Lord's the New Zealanders moved on to Northampton where their efforts in a drawn, weather-affected game tended to be overshadowed. The home side's Rob Bailey hit a powerful 95 off only 98 balls to offer a broad hint to the England selectors, and English newspapers were full of speculation about whether they would pick Botham for the Second Test as his ban was about to end. Few critics paid any attention to the unbeaten 100 scored by off-spinner John

Bracewell, but the New Zealander's second first-class century – his first had also been against English bowling for Auckland in 1984 – was a forerunner of heroics that were to decide the series.

In the event neither Botham nor Bailey was included in England's plans for Nottingham, but the Kiwis had seen enough of Bracewell's form down the order to include Stirling as an extra bowler in place of batsman Ken Rutherford. With a strengthened attack and valuable advice from Hadlee, who after a decade of playing at Trent Bridge for Nottinghamshire knew the pitch better than the back of his own hand, Coney asked England to bat first on winning the toss.

Encouraged by a standing ovation from his many local fans, overhead cloud and a sluggish pitch which hindered free stroke-play, Hadlee responded by putting England on the back foot from the word go. Graham Gooch, who had opened with three fine boundaries, attempted to clip a fourth through mid-wicket and was trapped lbw. Twenty-five minutes later Martyn Moxon was also heading in the direction of the pavilion after being bowled through the gate.

England enjoyed a brief spell on top as Hadlee's initial fire subsided, and Bill Athey and David Gower added 83 for the third wicket. Despite a general belief that Gower was mentally out of sorts after being stripped of the England captaincy early in the summer, he played with great freedom for 71 and only lost his wicket to a freak delivery – spinner Evan Gray turning the ball nearly two feet out of the bowler's rough to hit the stumps as the left-hander padded up. The England tail offered some spirited resistance through Greg Thomas and Bruce French, but when the innings closed on the second morning a total of 256 was hardly substantial and Hadlee's figures of six for 80 were no more than his efforts deserved.

Conditions were still in favour of the bowlers when the New Zealand innings began, but England's attack failed to make the most of them. Thomas was playing his first Test in England, Gladstone Small was making his debut and Derek Pringle, after four years of trying, had still to convince the critics of his international class, and their combined weaknesses and inexperience presented the tourists with a grand opportunity to force home the advantage.

That England managed to stay in contention for most of the second day was due more to the carelessness of the opposition than to the fruits of their own endeavours. The left-handed John Wright laid a

*John Emburey and Bruce French can only watch in awe as John Bracewell
hammers Phil Edmonds to the Trent Bridge ropes*

solid foundation, but having scored 58 in a shade over two hours he
lazily flicked Small into the hands of square leg, and Coney was
needlessly run out just before tea as he hesitated over a single. When,
shortly after the interval, Martin Crowe turned John Emburey into
the hands of backward short-leg, the New Zealanders, at 144 for 5,
appeared to have lost the advantage.

The match turned in two vital partnerships. First Hadlee and Gray
added 95 late on Friday night and early on Saturday to take the Kiwis
to within striking distance of the English total. Hadlee, proving once
again to be a fine all-rounder, dominated the stand striking eight
fours in a cultured 68. His departure, caught at slip off Thomas,
signalled the start of the finest day in Bracewell's cricketing career.

As the sun shone for the first time in the match on a packed Trent
Bridge Saturday crowd, the tall, gritty-faced twenty-six-year-old
totally ignored the danger posed by England taking the second new
ball. As Gray batted patiently towards his first Test half-century,
Bracewell set off towards his maiden Test hundred. At the start he
relied mainly on a series of searing drives, but four hours later as the

magical three figures began to approach he was brimming with enough confidence to pull and hook England's fast bowlers off the front foot, and gradually New Zealand's lead took on match-winning proportions. Although Gray eventually went to well-earned applause for a dogged 68, Bracewell found another willing ally in the youngster Stirling who helped add 65 for the ninth wicket. Bracewell was on 96 when Stirling departed bowled by Small, but Watson, fearing a lynch mob in the dressing room, hung around long enough to see Bracewell reach his coveted ton and then take New Zealand through to 413 all out for a lead of 157.

Coney clearly felt it was time to cash in on Bracewell's day of days. As the shadows began to lengthen he asked the off-spinner to bowl just one over, and during it he won an appeal for a bat–pad catch against Gooch which left England at 31 for 1 and in no mood to enjoy their Sunday off.

The wet weather had returned by Monday morning and with only 75 minutes' play possible there was nothing but frustration for the New Zealand side, who gloomily foresaw events from the First Test repeating themselves. But the rain relented on Tuesday and with Bracewell picking up the useful wickets of Athey and Gower, the England innings failed to gain momentum. There was unorthodox defiance from John Emburey, who played strange-looking shots from his own repertoire rather than the textbook on his way to a career-best 75, but after three dormant days by his own high standards Hadlee snapped back to life to take the last four England wickets, giving him ten in the match. With the home side dismissed for 230 New Zealand required just 74 to win, and although they lost Wright and Jeff Crowe cheaply, an historic victory was achieved with almost 8 of the last 20 overs to spare.

With England having suffered eight defeats in their last ten Tests, public demand for Botham's return in the Third and final Test at The Oval was overwhelming. The larger-than-life all-rounder duly took Bruce Edgar's wicket with his first ball back and later scored 59 not out, including equalling a record 24 runs in one over against Stirling. There were centuries, too, from Gower and Gatting, but rain played havoc with the game which ended in a dull draw, thus finally giving the Kiwis their first series victory in England at the tenth time of asking.

Dean Jones
Madras, 1986

There are few, if any, Test-match venues in the world that can equal the Chepauk Stadium in Madras for the physical strain it imposes on players. The Adelaide Oval is often just as hot and Calcutta's giant Eden Gardens just as humid, but the combination of both elements puts the Chepauk, a drab grey concrete bowl, near the bottom of the player comfort league table.

The Indians are wise enough not to play cricket at all in the height of summer with Madras lying barely 15 degrees north of the Equator, gently steaming on the south-western edge of the Bay of Bengal. But milder winter weather was barely on its way when the Australians, warming up for a forthcoming home Ashes series against Mike Gatting's England, visited the city in September 1986.

In comparison with their opponents, the Aussie squad was young and inexperienced. While the Indians could still field record-breaking opening batsman Sunil Gavaskar in the twilight of his career, and world-class all-rounder Kapil Dev, the visitors were attempting to rebuild after losing many senior players to a South African rebel tour. Skipper Allan Border was the only survivor of the previous Australian tour to the sub-continent in 1979 when the Indians won a six-match series two–nil, and his side was given little chance of gaining revenge.

Yet for five gruelling days Border's team fought brilliantly to produce one of the most gripping finishes in Test-cricket history, and from the game emerged a new Australian batting hero in the form of Dean Jones. Tall, slim and twenty-five years old, the former minor civil servant and sports goods salesman from Melbourne was struggling to establish himself in the Australian side and was chosen for the match ahead of Western Australia's Mike Veletta only on the toss of a coin.

Jones' cricketing pedigree had never been doubted. His father Barney, an aggressive all-rounder, had been something of a local legend as captain of Carlton, one of Melbourne's leading grade clubs. Throughout his childhood Jones spent many hours watching his father in action and at night would listen to the cricketing talk when other Carlton stars such as England fast bowler John Snow and Australian Test batsman Keith Stackpole visited the Jones household for a meal. But for all his background, when he first broke into the Australian side it was on the back of several dashing one-day performances for Victoria and his temperament for the five-day game was still very much under scrutiny by the time he arrived in Madras.

All the doubts, however, were dispelled on the first two days in the Chepauk when, playing in only his third Test, Jones contributed 210 towards the Australian first-innings total of 574 for 7 declared. Although he struck two sixes and twenty-seven fours during his nine-hour stay at the crease, it was not the big hitting which made his knock so memorable. It was the sheer determination he displayed to overcome fatigue and physical fitness, which led veteran Australian coach Bobby Simpson to declare: 'It was the gutsiest effort I have ever seen, one of the great double-centuries.'

Jones began his first Test innings on Indian soil with the game barely an hour old and the Australians, having chosen to bat first, at 48 for 1 having lost Geoff Marsh for 22 caught by Kapil Dev off the bowling of spinner Shivlal Yadav. For four and a half hours on that first day Jones played a secondary role alongside David Boon as the chunky Tasmanian scored 122 before falling to paceman Chetan Sharma with the new ball shortly before the close of play.

A tally at stumps of 56 not out said much for Jones' new-found patience against an Indian slow-bowling attack in which the off-spinner Yadav was supported by two left-armers in Ravi Shastri and Maninder Singh. But as he battled on into the second day Jones found he had much more than just his opponents to cope with, as he himself explained.

> The temperature was around 42 to 43 degrees Celsius, but on its own that did not worry me too much because I had batted in similar conditions in games at home. The bigger problem was the humidity which was registering over 90 per cent. There was a little bit of wind bringing air into the stadium, but that did not help at all since it was blowing from the direction of the canal at the side of the stadium where local people were dumping their sewage. The smell made me feel sick in the stomach and nauseous.
>
> I had gone into the match fully fit and by the end of the first, having batted four and a half hours and completed my first 50, I was feeling quite good. But it must have taken more out of me than I thought because

Dean Jones discovered that more than just the local curry was too hot in Madras

the next morning after only another hour at the crease I was absolutely wrecked and I knew I was in trouble.

As I was batting I started to vomit; then I started to get pins and needles which started in the fingers and gradually moved into my hands and arms, and as my condition got worse I twice urinated involuntarily in my pants. But I knew I had to keep going, and Sunil Gavaskar and all the Indian guys were fantastic; they could see I was in trouble but they all tried to encourage me to keep at it.

After he had completed his maiden Test century, Jones' condition deteriorated steadily. Although his team-mates forced him to take cold showers during the lunch and tea intervals he refused to consider leaving the field, and on his way to Australia's first ever double-century in India he compiled a 178-run stand for the fourth wicket with Allan Border, setting another record. But it was only a wicked taunt from his captain that kept Jones on the field as the afternoon wore on.

I was on about 167 when I finally said to AB that I had had enough. I was vomiting so often that I was holding the game up and I was so weak I was almost in a trance. But his response made me stay out there.

AB told me 'If you can't carry on then let's get a tough Queenslander out here who can handle the heat – a really good tough Australian, we'll get Fatcat [Greg Ritchie], he'll do the job.'

One mention of getting a Queenslander to do my job for me was enough. I told AB that I would carry on; I thought I'd show him.

But by tea, with 200 in his sights, Jones had reached new depths of physical exhaustion and broached the subject of retiring with Simpson. Eventually a compromise was reached whereby Jones agreed to carry on and just slog whatever extra runs he could.

Jones said 'I had got to the stage where I could no longer run. I'd told Simmo that I was hurt, so I went out and what followed was strange. I would block four balls, however good or bad they were, just to try and save up enough energy to have a go to hit the next one for four. They either went to the boundary or we walked a single. I couldn't go any faster.'

The new Victorian hero had been batting for 8 hours and 20 minutes when he was finally bowled by Yadav. He barely acknowledged a standing ovation as he walked painfully back to the pavilion, and once inside the dressing room he collapsed. Jones' condition was so severe that he was taken immediately to hospital and put on a saline drip to counter a bad case of dehydration. As he recalled later: 'Before the match I weighed 80 kg but by the end of the innings I was down to 72 kg, which meant I had lost well over a stone, and it was to take me another eight months before I got my weight back up to its right level.'

Although kept in hospital overnight, Jones returned to Chepauk the next day to take his place on the field for the rest of a match that was to capture cricket's imagination as it ended in only the second tie that had resulted from the 1052 Tests played up until that time.

Having completed his own Test century, Border closed Australia's first innings 37 minutes into the third day and then watched his own spinners take on the Indians at their own game. Young New South Wales off-spinner Greg Matthews took five for 103 as the Indians, with the help of 119 from Kapil Dev, just scrambled past the danger of following on to make 397.

Jones was fit enough to make 24 batting second time around as Australia made 170 for 5 in the 49 overs left for play on the fourth day before Border declared overnight and challenged the Indians to score 348 off 87 overs to win.

It was a sporting declaration, and with Gavaskar setting the pace with 90 and runs coming from most of the other top-order batsmen the Indians looked set for a spectacular victory. Suddenly, with only 18 runs needed off the last 5 overs, Australia gained the upper hand when Ray Bright dismissed both Chetan Sharma and Kiran More in quick succession. Yadav responded by swinging Matthews away for six, and with 7 runs wanted, two wickets in hand and still 2 overs to go, every form of result in the book was still on the cards. But while the situation called for cool heads, Yadav lost his and was bowled behind his legs by Bright as he aimed a reckless shot. The match finally climaxed with two balls to go when Maninder Singh fell lbw to Matthews and the scores finished level.

Test-match cricket had achieved only its second tie, to follow the match between Australia and the West Indies at Brisbane in 1960, and history will probably make the result the most memorable part of five steaming days in Chepauk. But for one very brave and exhausted young batsman it was the game where he finally came of age as a Test cricketer.

Abdul Qadir
Faisalabad, 1986

A common theme runs through the odd flashes of weakness displayed by the West Indies in the 1980s, which for the most part was a decade when they trampled underfoot all opposition with the subtlety of a steamroller under full power. Of the seventy-eight Tests played under the successive captaincies of Clive Lloyd and Viv Richards, only six ended in defeat – all of them on foreign soil and significantly five of them engineered by the fast-disappearing art of the spin bowler. In a way this was self-inflicted destruction for throughout the decade spinners virtually disappeared off the Caribbean scene, with even the smallest of islands relying on a non-stop diet of hostility from four big fast bowlers giving their batsmen little opportunity to take on the turning ball in their formative years. And as their main export to the English county system became pacemen, there were no longer as many openings as there had been for Gordon Greenidge and Richards in the seventies for Test batsmen to learn how to defy the spinners' guile overseas.

At Melbourne in 1981–82 when the West Indies lost to the Australians it was the tall, bounding off-spinner Bruce Yardley who did the damage in the second innings with four for 38; three years later in Sydney it was the grey-haired leg-spinner Bob Holland who became a match-winner with ten wickets in the match at a cost of 144. When Pakistan beat the West Indies in Faisalabad in 1985–86 they were undone by the wizardry of Abdul Qadir who took six for 16 in 9.3 overs. The only exception was at Christchurch in 1986–87, where Richards' men slumped to defeat at the hands of seamers Richard Hadlee, Ewen Chatfield and Martin Snedden with the Kiwis' lone spinner John Bracewell failing to take a single wicket. Their two other losses saw nineteen-year-old Indian leg-spinner Narendra Hirwani take sixteen wickets on his Test debut at Madras in 1987–88 and, the biggest shock of all, the performance of Australian skipper Allan Border in taking eleven for 96 with his rarely used orthodox slow left-arm spin against the West Indies at Sydney early in 1989.

Given that defeats for the West Indies were such rare occurrences throughout the decade, any one of those spinning performances merits inclusion here, but as a practitioner of slow-bowling skills Qadir, the son of a Muezzin – a Moslem official responsible for calling the faithful to their daily prayers – and a deeply religious man himself, stands out head and shoulders above the rest for his consistency as a Test-match performer.

Qadir first broke into the Pakistan side in the late seventies when, as with most Test nations, the mass defections to Kerry Packer's 'Cricket Circus' in Australia created numerous vacancies in official national sides. Having taken six for 67 on his first-class debut for the Punjab, he soon made an impact in the higher grade, taking six for 44 on only his second Test appearance at Hyderabad against Mike Brearley's 1977–78 tourists. In his early career he was protected from the spinners' graveyard of one-day cricket by a succession of Pakistani captains allowing him to develop his talents without the shackles imposed by the need for economy.

An excitable character, for whom flamboyant and prolonged appeals were to become a hallmark, Qadir was not always the flavour of the month with Pakistan's cricketing authorities, who once had cause to send him home from a tour to New Zealand. But he became a complete leg-spinner capable of mystifying the world's top batsmen. Apart from his stock ball, turning sharply away from the batsman, he developed a heavily disguised googly, two subtly different types of top-spinner and the 'flipper', a slower delivery which seemed to gather pace as it bounced but kept wickedly low. With such wonderful variety from a hand action which barely altered, Qadir became impossible to read. As England's Derek Randall admitted after scoring 105 against the Pakistanis at Edgbaston in 1982: 'I had no idea what was going on or which way Qadir was going to turn the ball next. I just got down on one knee and tried to smash everything over mid-wicket, and fortunately it came off on the day.'

Although Qadir's twirling fingers could extract prodigious spin from the most lifeless of wickets, it was often cruelly said that he was most effective on his own wickets in Pakistan where he was accused of being shown more than just a little favour by his local umpires. But after the West Indies astonishingly collapsed at Faisalabad late in October 1986, there were no complaints at the after-match press conference from either Richards or the West Indian tour manager Jackie Hendricks – each accepted with grace that they had been beaten by a truly worthy opponent.

The game had begun in the typically depressing fashion that was known only too well against West Indian opponents. Even though Michael Holding and Joel Garner had recently retired from the Test scene the tourists were still a frightening force with the new ball – Malcolm Marshall skidded in to dismiss the top three batsmen in the order, Qasim Omar trod on his stumps as he reeled back after being hit on his helmet by the lanky Tony Gray, and Salim Malik departed to hospital with a fractured wrist after another vicious rising delivery from Courtney Walsh homed in on its target with a sickening thud. It was only a fighting 61 from their skipper Imran Khan which enabled the Pakistanis to limp through to 159 all out.

Although Qadir and the off-spinner Tauseef Ahmed each took an early wicket it was the left-arm seam bowling of Wasim Akram, bowling off an efficient short run and moving the ball either way, which pegged back the West Indies batsmen. The young all-rounder took a career-best six for 91, while the tourists, hampered by a bout of stomach trouble which caused Richards to bat in some discomfort at number eight, responded with 248 for a lead of 89. By close of play on the second day Pakistan were in trouble as Marshall and Patrick Patterson had removed Mudassar Nazar and Rameez Raja cheaply for the second time in the match.

The third day developed into a war of attrition with Pakistan fighting desperately against a barrage of bouncers and making the most of a series of lucky escapes. As opener Mohsin Khan made 40 and night-watchman Salim Yousuf a brave 61, several involuntary strokes sent the ball into the air only to land in empty spaces without a fielder, but the unrelenting pace gradually took its toll as Pakistan collapsed to 224 for 7. Late in the day, however, and into the fourth morning they were revived by Imran following up his first-innings half-century with a steady 23 and then by an astonishing last-wicket partnership between Wasim Akram and Salim Malik. The latter batted with one arm cast in plaster and knowing that another blow on the wrist could inflict lasting damage. But with Wasim smashing both Marshall and Gray over mid-wicket for six and Salim bravely fending off fourteen deliveries, they added 32 valuable runs to take Pakistan to 328 all out, setting the West Indies a victory target of 240 in four full sessions.

After only one of those sessions, however, their innings was in complete disarray. Imran gave his first-innings destroyer Wasim

Abdul Qadir – capable of bamboozling the best

Akram just 3 overs before turning to Qadir as the wicket began to crumble. Imran himself struck first, trapping both the West Indies openers Desmond Haynes and Greenidge lbw before Qadir got down to work.

The highly dependable Larry Gomes was undone by an almost unplayable googly, delivered from wide of the crease, which pitched over two feet outside the off stump before turning back in to strike middle. Richards, still feeling out of sorts, was caught close to the wicket along with Richie Richardson, who could only lay his bat handle on a ball which turned and lifted. As Imran again interceded to have Jeff Dujon lbw, Qadir produced his flipper which kept low to creep under the bat of the 6 foot 6 inches tall Roger Harper, and he deceived Gray in the flight with a yorker.

An incredible game ended twenty minutes into the final morning when Qadir bent down on one knee to accept a low return catch from Marshall, and Pakistan had won by 186 runs.

Astonishingly, in only 25 overs the West Indies, kings of cricket, had been bowled out for 53, their lowest ever Test score and 23 fewer than their previous worst, made also against Pakistan at Dacca in 1958–59. It was the first time Richards had experienced a defeat as Test captain, and it ended a run of seven successive West Indian victories.

Peter Taylor
Sydney, 1987

Many Australian cricket-lovers must have had a jolly good chuckle at the selectors' expense when they picked through the newspaper headlines over breakfast on the morning of 7 January 1987. The national team was in a state of crisis having already lost the Ashes to England two Tests to nil with one to play, and a special four-nation cricketing jamboree in Perth arranged to coincide with the America's Cup yacht race was to be in England's pocket later that day. There was, however, still to be played the Fifth and final Ashes Test at Sydney, and the papers were full of news about the Aussies' team selection.

'Peter Who?' was the overwhelming reaction to the news that Peter Taylor, an off-spinner who was second in line for a place in the New South Wales state side behind the ever-popular Greg Matthews, was in line to make his Test debut. Surely it was a mistake and the selectors had meant to summon up his NSW team-mate Mark Taylor, a left-handed opening batsman who could have filled the large gap that had opened in the side during the previous weeks as Tasmanian David Boon gradually had his confidence eroded by England's pacemen. Peter Taylor was a thirty-year-old agricultural scientist who had played just four Sheffield Shield games and taken only eight wickets, but the selectors insisted they had got the right man, and the move had turned out to be pure inspiration.

Taylor had in fact made a small impact a year earlier while touring Zimbabwe with New South Wales, when in two matches he took eleven wickets against the host nation. But it was not the sort of form to warrant elevation to Test status and it seems more likely that Greg Chappell, the former Australian captain, had actually plucked the rabbit out of the hat. Chappell had been impressed by Taylor in the 1986 Sheffield Shield final when he took four for 31 against Queensland, and had tried to persuade the spinner to move to the Sunshine State where there would have been greater opportunities for him at first-class level. Although Taylor had declined the move, Chappell, it is widely assumed, had not forgotten his talents and with Australian cricket in disarray, desperate times called for desperate measures.

The Australians had started the summer of 1986–87 in somewhat buoyant mood, having begun their preparations for England's visit by undertaking a short tour to India. Despite recurrent health problems they had emerged from a three-Test series on the subcontinent with two creditable draws and the distinction of having taken part in only the second tied Test in history. Geoff Marsh and David Boon had begun to establish a trusty opening partnership, Dean Jones had emerged as a middle-order batsman for the future after his 210 at Madras, and the tall, awkward Bruce Reid, a left-handed paceman, gave hopes of future strength on the bowling side.

The English, on the other hand, arrived Down Under trying to shake off a depressing run of eight defeats and three draws in their previous eleven Tests. They had a new management structure, with Micky Stewart on trial for the position of full-time coach and in captain Mike Gatting a leader full of pugnacious qualities. Compared with the Australians the team had a wealth of experience, as David Gower at the time had 86 caps, Ian Botham 85, and both Allan Lamb and Gatting approaching half-centuries. But their progress in the early state warm-up games was alarming, as one batting failure followed another and defeat at the hands of Queensland was almost followed by similar embarrassment against Western Australia. Their form suggested to Martin Johnson, cricket correspondent of the newly launched *Independent* newspaper, that England 'can't bat, can't bowl, can't field', as the first Test approached in Brisbane.

As it turned out, Johnson was quickly made to eat his words. As Ian Botham played one of the most disciplined innings of his career to score 138 not out at Brisbane, and Graham Dilley, after years of injuries and unfulfilled promise, took five wickets in a Test innings for the first time, Australia were forced to follow on and England turned the form book upside down with victory by seven wickets.

Johnson was later to admit: 'The comments were right; I just referred to the wrong team!' England's superiority was confirmed in the second Test in which only a fighting 125 from Allan Border saved his side from the ignominy of following on again, and even though the Australians scored 514 batting first in the Third Test at Adelaide, it was on a featherbed batting track and the visitors had few problems securing a draw to maintain their lead in the series.

The Ashes issue was decided in the Fourth Test which began at Melbourne on Boxing Day and ended shortly after tea three days

Umpire Steve Randall laughs but England found nothing amusing about Peter Taylor's bowling on his Test debut

later, with England the victors by an innings and 14 runs. The week-long sojourn to Perth for the America's Cup challenge gave the Australian selectors time to draw breath, though England's victory in Western Australia seemed only to confirm the gap in class that had emerged between the two sides by the time they arrived at Sydney to conclude the Test series.

The widely held conviction that the selectors had indeed picked the wrong Taylor appeared to be confirmed when the Australians batted first using Greg Ritchie, the stocky middle-order batsman from Queensland, as a makeshift opening partner for Geoff Marsh. That particular move failed to work, but with Dean Jones scoring 184 not out – though England were convinced he was caught behind down the leg side when he had made only 5 – the Aussies were more than content with a total of 343 on a pitch that was not expected to last. Additionally so because apart from Taylor, the Aussies had also chosen leg-spinner Peter Sleep in their line-up.

Taylor had made an early impact with the bat, keeping Jones company for 84 valuable minutes while scoring 11 towards the end of the Aussie innings, but his bowling turned out to be the find of the season. In a rare occurrence in the series, Broad failed as both he and Bill Athey fell cheaply to the pace of Merv Hughes, and Gatting fell lbw to Reid without scoring. England began to pull round in a fourth-wicket partnership between Gower and Lamb which raised 72 runs, but then Taylor struck.

Although Lamb was his first victim caught behind by Tim Zoehrer as he attempted to cut, it was the wicket of Ian Botham that gave him the greatest early satisfaction. The all-rounder had tried to dominate him from the start, powerfully despatching his first two deliveries to the off-side boundary. But the tall, red-haired, quietly spoken spinner was not easily scared. Although Botham thumped him for a huge six which sailed through the England dressing-room window in his next over, barely a dozen further deliveries had passed before the England hero was on his way back in the same direction, caught by Marsh at short leg while trying to drive. On the third morning Taylor made sure that England were going to struggle to get anywhere near level terms in the first innings. David Gower had batted stubbornly for 72 but as he went for a cover-drive, Taylor deceived him in the flight and Dirk Wellham took the catch.

Just as the Australian tail had thwarted England on the second morning, finishing off the visitors proved as difficult. Jack Richards and John Emburey added 71 for the seventh wicket and Emburey and Small 51 for the ninth, all three employing the most frustrating of tactics against the newcomer. England were well aware that Australian umpires will not willingly give batsmen out lbw on the front foot, and so for over after over the Sydney crowd and the

His battling had to be taken seriously as well

Australian bowlers were infuriated by the sight of batsmen planting the left pad well down the wicket with little intention of playing a shot. However, patience paid off for Taylor as he eventually bowled Emburey and Small, and by having Phil Edmonds picked up at short leg off bat and pad he finished with six for 78 from 26 highly respectable overs – some performance from a player who had expected to spend the weekend playing grade cricket. And still he wasn't finished.

Although the Australians had secured a first-innings lead of 68 they were by no means in the clear when England's two much more established spinners – Emburey and Edmonds – got to work on a deteriorating pitch second time around. Although Emburey had needed a runner during England's first innings he was still able to bowl despite a groin strain which restricted his follow-through, and in the best spell of his long career he reduced the Australians to 145 for 7. That was the cue for Taylor to resume his heroics. With youngster Steve Waugh still finding his way in the Australian side there was no guarantee the second innings would not fold quickly, but the pair pieced together a 98-run stand that first survived against the spinners and then even picked up momentum when Gatting turned to the new ball to try to force a breakthrough. Taylor contributed 42, and given that he batted for a total of 244 minutes in his two innings it was no mean effort for a player batting at nine on his Test debut.

History was very much on the Australians' side when England went to the wicket for a second time needing 320 to win, since they had only once previously scored more than 300 batting fourth to win a Test match and that had been back in the 1928–29 season at Melbourne. Yet they added to the appeal of a thoroughly fascinating Test match by falling only 55 runs short. Much of that was due to Gatting's captain's innings of 96, with added support from Richards and Emburey. It was the leg-spin of Sleep that saw the Aussies past the post; he took five for 72 as England were bowled out for 264.

Taylor also made another valuable contribution by claiming the wickets of Lamb and Botham, for the second time in the match, in 29 overs, which helped Sleep keep pressure on the English batsmen. Total match figures of eight for 154, 53 valuable runs and the prized scalp of Botham twice were more than anyone could have expected from Taylor on his Test debut. There was no other candidate for the Man of the Match award, and by the next morning newspaper readers throughout Australia had found the answer to 'Peter Who?'

Allan Lamb
Sydney, 1987

Although by mid January 1987 England's winter tourists in Australia under the astute leadership of Mike Gatting had already won the Ashes and the America's Cup challenge in Perth, their chances of completing a grand slam Down Under by lifting the World Series Cup one-day competition were not highly rated.

Their opponents in the annual triangular competition were the West Indies who, after frequent winter visits, had come to regard the rich pickings of Australian prize money as their own, and the Australian side which, despite its poor Test form, was vastly experienced in the limited-over field and were to go on to win the World Cup in India ten months later. In the round-robin pre-final qualifying matches the early results reflected the closeness of the competition, with England beating the West Indies, Australia beating England and the West Indies beating Australia.

England's second meeting with the Aussies was scheduled to take place under floodlights at Sydney where the home side had won the final Test of the winter barely a fortnight earlier, and the thrills and spills of the one-day game had rekindled local interest. A vast crowd at the Sydney Cricket Ground saw Australia reach 233 for 8 off their 50 overs, mainly due to a solid innings of 97 from Dirk Wellham, and their hopes of a home victory were boosted as England's batsmen floundered in the mid-light between the afternoon sun and the floodlights taking over.

Chris Broad, scourge of the Aussies all season, made 45 and David Gower a neat half-century, but wickets fell regularly to the extent that England needed 18 off the final over to clinch victory. The last six balls were to be delivered by the pencil-slim, tall, blond figure of Bruce Reid, a left-arm fast bowler whose height and swing made him an awkward proposition and the Australians firm favourites.

But Allan Lamb at the other end had ideas which were to turn the result upside down. On his way to 59 not out Lamb had not thus far batted with great authority, and his opening shot in the last over to deep extra cover was rewarded with 2 runs only as the result of a wild throw. He gained confidence by hitting the next ball to square leg for

Bruce Reid walks away in dismay after Allan Lamb has secured a remarkable win for England under the Sydney floodlights

four, and sent English confidence sky high with a pick-up against the third ball which was deposited a dozen rows back in the stands at deep mid-wicket.

As a previously buoyant Australian crowd began to cower in fear, Lamb struggled against the fourth delivery, guiding it to cover for a single, but England picked up an extra run from an overthrow and won the game off the fifth delivery which Lamb blasted away to the square-leg boundary.

It was an improbable victory which sent England to the top of the WSC qualifying table, and within a fortnight Gatting's team had beaten Australia twice in the finals to complete a unique hat-trick of titles. The tide had definitely swung in their favour with Lamb's innings, which was based on a simple philosophy. He said afterwards: 'In one-day cricket nothing is impossible, but you must never give up.' And it was that determination that put paid to Reid and Australia in Sydney.

Notts *v.* Northants
NatWest Trophy, 1987

At 7.15 p.m. on Saturday 15 September 1987 umpires David Shepherd and Alan Whitehead were faced with a great temptation. Clouds and drizzle had long since knocked the shine off the NatWest Trophy final between Northamptonshire and Nottinghamshire, which had been traditionally billed as a showcase ending to the domestic English season. What should have been a close encounter between two sides packed with Test stars and young talent had deteriorated into a one-sided affair. A game reduced by the elements to 50 overs a side had seen Northants, when asked to bat first, score 228 for 3 and then Nottinghamshire collapse dramatically against the pace of Winston Davis to 57 for 4 off 21 overs in reply.

Messrs Shepherd and Whitehead simply had to decide whether a result could be achieved on the Saturday night – and with Nottinghamshire in total disarray it certainly looked that way – or whether to drag both teams back down to London to finish off the game in front of empty stands on the Monday morning. Shepherd later recalled: 'The result didn't seem to be in doubt since Notts had collapsed, but it was September and we thought it would be dark before another 29 overs had been bowled so we didn't have much choice.' And for that bit of logical thinking and a great innings by Richard Hadlee, Nottinghamshire will always be grateful.

When the two sides reassembled at Lord's on the Monday morning, most members of the 25,000 Saturday crowd were back at work and there were barely a thousand people scattered among the huge stands to witness Northants' seemingly inevitable march to victory. Light rain delayed the restart by an hour, and when play did get under way Nottinghamshire's South African skipper Clive Rice was hard pressed to make any headway. Although he was to score 63, 39 of his runs came from singles as the ball struggled to make progress over a sodden outfield. When he was out mistiming a drive against the spin of Richard Williams to Geoff Cook at mid-on, it seemed just another nail in Nottinghamshire's coffin.

Nottinghamshire then wanted a further 83 runs from only 8.5 overs and Hadlee, playing his last major one-day innings before retiring

Richard Hadlee celebrates after leading Notts to victory in the 1987 NatWest Trophy final

from county cricket, had no guarantee of support at the other end from Bruce French, who had scored only 7 runs in three previous NatWest knocks that summer.

Northamptonshire skipper Cook had used Nottinghamshire's need for defence on the Saturday night to get through the overs of his spinner Nick Cook and Richard Williams cheaply, but he hadn't quite completed the task. Williams had one more to bowl – the 44th of the innings – and Hadlee used it to change the course of the match dramatically. His first ball flew for six through the outstretched hands of Allan Lamb at mid-wicket. The second might also have given Rob Bailey a chance at long-on, but he lost the ball in the sun as the batsmen ran two and Lamb did marvellously to stop the third going for another boundary. In all, 15 runs flowed from the over and Nottinghamshire were on the march.

West Indian Davis returned to the Northants attack to try to stem the tide, but found that French had taken his cue from Hadlee and was playing with confidence. A target of 51 off 5 overs was reduced to 8 off the last, to be bowled by David Capel who was suffering from a back strain. With Hadlee rampant the Northants seamer would have struggled to survive even at full fitness.

Although French was unluckily run out off the first ball, Hadlee struck the second for a straight six at the Nursery End and then pulled the third to the Tavern boundary to complete a stunning victory with three balls to spare. Hadlee's unbeaten 70 had come off only sixty-one balls, with two sixes and four fours, and given his match-winning partnership with French of 75 in only 8 overs, there was no other candidate for Man of the Match.

Graeme Hick
Taunton, 1988

Although the legendary Victorian cricketer Dr W. G. Grace achieved the feat twice in 1876, only a further 97 triple-centuries have been scored in first-class cricket since. In more recent times as the standard of wickets worldwide has deteriorated and bowlers have tended to take more time delivering their overs, occurrences have become even rarer.

The 1980s saw six new batsmen add their names to the list of scores above 300 – New Zealanders Glenn Turner and Ken Rutherford, West Indian Viv Richards, Australian David Hookes, Pakistan's Abdul Azeem and Zimbabwe's Graeme Hick – but only one of them was able to take his innings into an even higher plane by passing 400. That honour belonged to Hick who, seventeen days before his twenty-second birthday, took advantage of the introduction of four-day cricket in England's County Championship by making 405 not out for Worcestershire against Somerset at Taunton in May 1988.

Hick had been spotted as a boy wonder when visiting England with Zimbabwe's 1983 World Cup squad as a talented seventeen-year-old, and was persuaded to join Worcestershire as an overseas player with the long-term objective of qualifying to play Test cricket for England. Sharing the overseas spot with Kapil Dev in 1985, Hick scored two Championship centuries; given a full season in 1986 he made 1934 runs with six centuries; and the following season there were another eight three-figure scores in his overall tally of 1868.

To all who saw him in action it had become obvious that the strapping 6 foot 3 inch blond-haired right-hander was destined for the top. But given that he was asked by England to wait ten years – later reduced to seven – before making the Test arena, some critics feared that Hick might become bored with run-of-the-mill county cricket and lose his appetite for runs. In five sunny sessions at Taunton he provided the answer. The bare statistics show that he faced 469 balls in 555 minutes, striking eleven sixes and thirty-three fours, and while he was said to have survived sharp chances at 67, 101 and 141 it was only a declaration from Worcestershire's captain Phil Neale that brought relief to the Somerset bowlers.

Somerset's Nick Felton takes evasive action as Graeme Hick finds the boundary yet again during his innings of 405 at Taunton

Although Hick had made the highest score on English soil in the twentieth century, and only eight bigger innings have been played in first-class cricket in history, Neale admitted later that he had not realised Hick was only 19 runs short of Archie MacLaren's Championship record score made for Lancashire, coincidentally also at Taunton against Somerset, in 1895.

The demands made on a cricketer scoring 400 are immense; batting for nine and a quarter hours requires enormous reserves of stamina. But Hick showed no sign of wavering, and no one suffered more during the innings than Peter Roebuck, the Somerset captain, whose job it was to try to stem the flow of runs. Asked to describe the innings later in *Wisden Cricketers' Almanac*, Roebuck wrote:

Once or twice his leg shots were lifted, but they were hit with a power that was efficient rather than savage and they thundered through or over the field. Standing erect and immense yet never imperious Hick boomed drives to mid-off or through extra cover – 'not a man move' shots – and he late cut delicately. Throughout he ran fast between the wickets, throughout he used a bat so broad that bowlers felt they were trying to knock down a tank with a pea-shooter.

Roebuck later added: 'At the crease Hick avoided flamboyance and eschewed the macho. Discipline was at the core of his game. If he was bowled a good ball he blocked it. Bad balls were hit.'

The innings set Hick up to join the elite band of players who had completed a thousand first-class runs before the end of May, and in a blazing summer he scored a total of ten centuries, including two other doubles. A total of 2713 runs at an average of 77.51 emphatically proved that Hick was not losing his appetite in county crcket – though many bowlers wished he had.

Combined Universities
Benson & Hedges Cup, 1989

One of the more bizarre excuses offered for the decline in English cricket in the 1980s dated back to the abandonment of National Service. It was claimed in some quarters that two years in the forces had produced older students attending university and therefore more mature cricketers better equipped to take on the counties.

It was a somewhat dubious argument, since both Oxford and Cambridge had gradually placed greater emphasis on academic achievement rather than sporting prowess and had thus weakened their representative sides. Thus, with their first-class status under constant pressure, the decision in 1987 to enter a combined side from all British universities for the first time in the Benson and Hedges Cup was to prove far-sighted. By the summer of 1989 they were able to field a team containing ten players who had signed to play for

Nasser Hussain showed no respect for Somerset with his brilliant century for the Combined Universities in 1989

counties on completion of their courses, and they proceeded to take the competition by storm.

Surrey visited Fenner's early in May and were beaten by 9 runs as they failed to overhaul a target of 117 in 37 overs. Then Mike Gatting put the students back in their place with 123 not out as the Universities lost their second qualifying game to Middlesex at Oxford by eight wickets. But under the astute leadership of Mike Atherton, and with the benefit for team morale of a short tour to the West Country, the students bounced straight back.

At Worcester they had to cope with stars such as Ian Botham, Graham Dilley and Graeme Hick, but, led by a 67 from Nasser Hussain, they overhauled a target of 217 to win by five wickets. Their final qualifying match at Bristol resulted in a tense last-over defeat at the hands of Gloucestershire, but Atherton's team had already done enough to edge into the quarter-finals for the first time, ahead of Middlesex on run rate with Worcestershire and Surrey both also failing to qualify.

The quarter-final draw took the Universities to Taunton where the locals, despite a previous diet of heroics from players of the standing of Botham, Viv Richards and Joel Garner, packed the picturesque ground in the hope of an upset. It looked as if they would be disappointed as Somerset's South African find of the summer, Jimmy Cook, and Peter Roebuck put on a century for the county's first wicket and the 200 was passed with only two wickets down. With Roebuck scoring 102, a total of 252 looked far in excess of the students' capabilities, especially since exams had robbed them of opener Steve James. To make matters worse, their innings was barely a dozen overs old before Mark Crawley was taken to hospital with a cracked knuckle.

But Atherton and Nasser Hussain took the Universities through to 78 without further drama until shortly before tea, when the captain was out for 26. Somerset were then rocked back on their heels as Hussain and John Longley, who crashed 49 off only 39 balls, put on 114 in only 17 overs to set the match alight. Their efforts meant that only 31 were needed off the last 5 overs with six wickets in hand, but a rash of wickets coincided with Hussain losing his previously fluent timing and although only 9 were wanted off the last over, bowled by Roebuck, Somerset were spared embarrassment with a 3-run victory.

The Universities, however, had made people sit up and take notice for the first time in years.

Eddie Hemmings
Benson & Hedges Cup, 1989

History threatened to repeat itself as the 1989 Benson and Hedges Cup final at Lord's between Essex and Nottinghamshire built up into a thrilling climax. Four years earlier when the two teams had clashed in the NatWest Trophy final, Essex had edged home by the slenderest of margins – 1 run – when, with two needed off the last delivery from Derek Pringle, former England Test batsman Derek Randall could only steer the ball into the waiting hands of Paul Prichard at mid-wicket.

A similar nail-biting finale was on the cards in 1989 when Essex, the Cup favourites, asked Nottinghamshire to score 244 in 55 overs. The Midlands side were always around and about the required scoring rate, thanks to 86 from their skipper Tim Robinson and 54 from Paul Johnson. And they looked set to overturn the form book as Randall, desperate to atone for 1985, scored a breathtaking 49. But when he

Jubilant Notts fans mob Eddie Hemmings and Bruce French after the last ball victory in the 1989 Benson and Hedges Cup final

was caught on the leg-side boundary – again off the bowling of Pringle – in the penultimate over, Nottinghamshire, with no more specialist batsmen to follow, looked set to fall at the last hurdle again.

With a packed 25,000 crowd perched on the edges of their seats, the last over developed into a classic confrontation between the two oldest players on the field. Desperate to prevent Nottinghamshire from scoring the 9 they needed to win, Essex were able to call upon John Lever to bowl. At forty years of age and with twenty-three years' cricketing experience at the highest level, the left-arm paceman was the ideal man for the job. Facing him was Eddie Hemmings, born four days earlier than Lever in February 1949 but regarded as a specialist off-spinner rather than a batsman, even though he had once scored 95 in a Test against Australia.

Scampered singles, a bye to the wicket-keeper, two runs to the boundary in front of the famous Tavern Stand, and a ball from which it was impossible to score led to Hemmings facing the last ball of the game with 4 runs wanted. Tension grew as Essex skipper Graham Gooch carefully set his field to cater for Lever bowling a yorker-length ball aimed at Hemmings' leg stump. He decided to pack the leg-side boundary, leaving Hemmings with the almost impossible task of steering the ball backward of point to find the largest gap in the off-side field.

Summoning up all the control that he had acquired through his vast experience, Lever duly delivered the perfect yorker. But to the unfettered joy of the Nottinghamshire supporters, Hemmings gave himself room, sliced the ball wide of Brian Hardie fielding at square cover, and found the ropes in front of the Lord's Grandstand only a second ahead of the pursuing fielder. Hemmings and his partner Bruce French then performed a victory dance in the middle of the pitch, after having pulled off a most remarkable and well-deserved victory.

Mark Taylor
Ashes Series, 1989

As the 1989 Ashes series in England approached, with the two oldest enemies in cricket still thought to be lagging way behind the West Indies in terms of world rankings, there was much speculation about the make-up of the two sides.

The English camp was in a state of transformation. The previous winter's tour to India had been aborted because of political oppositon to the South African connections of skipper Graham Gooch and several other members of the tour party, and early in the year Ted Dexter had been appointed the first chairman of the newly formed England Committee. One of his first decisions, after his initial choice of Mike Gatting was vetoed, was to replace Gooch as captain with David Gower, who believed that England's best chance of hanging on to the coveted urn lay with older more experienced players such as Gooch, Allan Lamb and Ian Botham – although many critics felt that the time had come for the introduction of fresh young talent.

As the Australian touring party was announced at the end of a season in which they had lost a Test series to the West Indies, most of the arguments focused on the pace-bowling attack. Would big, bustling and aggressive Merv Hughes be effective on slower English wickets? Why was the New South Wales left-arm seamer Mike Whitney omitted after a highly successful Sheffield Shield season? And just exactly who was Greg Campbell, a youngster from Tasmania who made the trip after playing barely a handful of first-class games? In England, at least, little attention was paid to the inclusion of the left-handed New South Wales opening batsman Mark Taylor. It seemed obvious to outside observers that the Australians would not break up a powerful batting line launched by new openers Geoff Marsh and David Boon and backed up by established stars Dean Jones and Allan Border, with the promising Steve Waugh at number five. Taylor, after all, had made a total of only 67 runs in his first two Tests against the West Indies at Sydney and Adelaide. Yet before the blazing English summer of 1989 was over he was a household name at both ends of the world.

There was no doubt that Taylor deserved his place in the

Australian party. Prior to his debut against the West Indies he had not made a hundred in state cricket all season, although he had passed 80 five times. But he finished the Australian summer in glorious style for New South Wales, scoring three centuries and totalling over 600 runs in their last four games. The big question in his own mind was whether he had done enough to split the established Marsh and Boon opening partnership. He recalled later:

> I had been fairly confident of making the tour party, having done fair to middling in my first two Tests against the West Indies. But I knew that to get into the Australian side against England as an opener I was always going to have to do a fair bit more. Over of the preceding couple of years David Boon and Geoff Marsh had become a very good opening partnership. They got on well together, they roomed together and they ran well together at the wicket. I had been picked for the tour because of my consistency over the previous season and I thought my best chance of playing in the Test might have been to bat at three. But one of the reasons why I got to open was that our coach Bobby Simpson had always felt very big about the need to rotate the strike – never letting a bowler get on top of one particular batsman.
>
> From my early days at New South Wales when Simmo had also been the coach there he always impressed upon me that even if I was scoring fours every over I should not forget about the singles – they kept bowlers guessing. And the other thing in my favour was that I was a left-hander and the left and right opening combination has the same effect on bowlers. If I had been Mark Taylor, a right-handed batsman, and had had a similar consistent season with New South Wales, I don't think I would have been picked for the tour in the first place.

In fact Taylor had one other major factor going for him when the Australian selectors drew up their blueprint for the tour. He had proved himself an outstanding slip fielder, and with new-ball bowlers Terry Alderman and Geoff Lawson always likely to get movement under English conditions, it was vital that the tourists had someone at slip capable of taking catches off the edge of the bat. Taylor was to take five in the series with only Boon, fielding most at short leg, and wicket-keeper Ian Healy managing more.

Taylor failed to make the Australian side for the Texaco Trophy one-day internationals, which ended with a win apiece for both sides and a thrilling tie at Nottingham with England being declared the winners of the series under a complicated and near farcical situation

Tim Curtis said 'ouch' for the whole of England as he tried to evade a typical Mark Taylor square drive at Old Trafford in 1989

where the tie was reassigned as an English victory two days after the game had been played. But when the two teams assembled at Headingley early in June for the First Test, Simpson and skipper Allan Border had decided to break up the Boon–Marsh opening combination as Taylor responded in magnificent style. His maiden Test century came in the first innings when he scored 136, and he followed it with 60 off only 112 balls in the second innings as Australia went one–nil up in the six-match series. At Lord's in the Second Test he made 62 and 27 in another Australian victory, but all his efforts were overshadowed by Steve Waugh who scored stunning unbeaten centuries in both games.

Later Taylor admitted that all the attention and headlines devoted to his colleague did him a huge favour.

Steve batted really well and when he scores 100 or 150 with his style he's capable of overshadowing anyone. But that didn't worry me; in fact, it might have helped a bit. I don't think the English bowlers were thinking that much about me. They thought, 'Here we've got Mark Taylor; we don't know a lot about him – he's played a couple of Tests against the West Indies, but he didn't do particularly well.' I think they were concentrating more on working out the weaknesses and strengths of people like Boon, Marsh, Border and Jones. To a certain extent they had seen Steve a bit in the past, but the result was that we two ended up being the best batsmen in the series.

Taylor was by no means a failure in the drawn Third Test at Birmingham where he contributed 43 and 51, and he made a further significant contribution with 85 in the first innings of the fourth match at Old Trafford. But his first big emotional moment came in the second innings when he was at the crease on the final day with 37 not out as Boon swept the boundary which gave Australia the Ashes. He said: 'Even though we had gone two–nil up early in the series and things had been rather easy for us – we hadn't looked like losing – there was still a big sense of relief when Boony hit those runs. Even if it was easy and the West Indies were still regarded as the best side in the world, an Ashes series is still the biggest thing in cricket and we had done what we set out to do.'

By the end of the Manchester Test England were in complete disarray. Tabloid newspapers were screaming for the head of David Gower on a plate, while the home selectors were in complete turmoil when it was announced in Johannesburg that sixteen of the country's top players had signed contracts to join a rebel tour to South Africa in 1990. It was immediately announced by Lord's that the rebels would not be considered for the final two Tests and England, having already discarded several failures early on and lost Allan Lamb to a series of injuries, went in search of a new team. The only danger to the Australians as they approached the final two Tests appeared to come from inside their own camp. They turned out to be far too professional to allow the victory celebrations and hangovers to last for ever, and any thoughts of Border's team relaxing for the Fifth Test at Trent Bridge were extinguished as Taylor's brilliant summer reached even greater heights.

After Border had won the toss Taylor and Marsh put on 329 for the first wicket, rewriting the record books in the process. And doubters who felt that both the Australian openers were somewhat limited in style and flair were made to eat their words as the pair scored 301 without being parted on the opening day.

Taylor celebrating his first ton during a record-breaking opening stand of 329 with Geoff Marsh at Nottingham

For the first time in the history of Test cricket in England a crowd was forced to sit through a complete day's play watching the same two batsmen in action and without a wicket falling. It was a measure of Taylor's growing confidence that he played through a fairly shaky pre-lunch period when the English bowlers, given a modicum of luck, might just have reaped some rewards for their efforts. Early on Taylor was troubled by the genuine pace of Devon Malcolm, the Derbyshire fast bowler who was making his debut. And when he had made only 3 he edged Angus Fraser towards Martyn Moxon at slip, but the chance went begging. In the period before lunch he also edged Ian Botham uppishly in the region of the slips, but nothing went to hand and he made England pay dearly. Taylor commented: 'There were also a couple of shouts of lbw, but as the innings grew I realised that luck was probably on my side and I decided to make the most of it.'

Fired by that resolve, Taylor, along with Marsh, set about changing the record books as cricket's army of statisticians were forced into overtime. Throughout his career Marsh, the solidly built Western Australian, had built his game on a sound technique backed by a limited range of scoring shots. Taylor, equally stocky in stature, proved to be more adventurous. Playing basically with his head over the line and displaying nimble footwork, he was at his best driving forcefully through the covers whenever the English bowlers over-pitched – an occurrence which increased in frequency as the partnership grew.

And so the records tumbled in turn. By the time Marsh departed for 138 at 12.12 p.m. on the second day, caught off spinner Nick Cook, the pair had put on 329, a new record for either side in an Ashes Test and the fourth highest opening partnership in all Test cricket. It was also the best opening stand in any Test in England.

England might have been relieved to see Marsh disappear up the pavilion steps at Trent Bridge, but another 81 runs were to be added before a weary Taylor, after nine and a quarter hours at the crease, stepped down the wicket to Cook and was smartly stumped by Jack Russell for 219. He had completed his first ever double-century in any form of first-class cricket and had become the first Australian to score more than 200 against England for eighteen and a half years.

After such a start the Australians had complete control of the match, though Border chose to bat on until well into the third day before declaring at 602 for 6. England's response, facing the daunting task of scoring over 400 just to save the follow-on, was a continuing story in a summer of disasters. They were bowled out for 255 and 167, mainly falling to the guile of Terry Alderman, and a victory by an innings and 180 meant that the 1989 Australians had become only the second touring side from Down Under to win four Tests in a series in England, following in the footsteps of Don Bradman's 1948 team.

Given all his many achievements in the game either side of the Second World War, few would have thought that by the end of the summer Bradman's name would have been linked so often with Taylor's. The reason was simple. As the team went to The Oval for the Sixth Test Taylor had already amassed 726 runs in the series, and in Ashes terms only one player had ever scored more for Australia – The Don himself. Bradman had set the all-time record of 974 fifty-nine years earlier, and for all Taylor's outstanding achievements in the preceding months it was far too much to ask for him to score another 248 runs in the final Test, although he made a brave attempt. With Australia again batting first he made 71 and followed up with 48 second time around.

The net result was a reward of 839 runs from the summer at an average of 83.90 and two of Bradman's other records – 758 runs in 1934 and 810 in 1936–37 – now tucked in behind his own name. And Taylor, who had slipped almost unnoticed into England with the touring party early in May, found himself a national hero when he and the rest of the team were given a tickertape reception on their return to his native Sydney in September.

Jack Russell
Old Trafford, 1989

In the thirteen years between 1968 and 1981 the England selectors were afforded one major luxury in the shape of Alan Knott. As a world class wicket-keeper he broke all previous English Test records, but he was also able to offer one other invaluable asset to a succession of captains. While the equally brilliant glovework of Bob Taylor often challenged Knott for his Test place, the Kent player was always able to fight it off through his ability with the bat. As an acknowledged number seven of right with a sound defence, limitless powers of concentration and cheekily improvised attacking play, Knott scored 4389 runs in ninety-five Tests at an average of 32.75 including five hundreds. So when in 1981, at the age of thirty-five, Knott announced that he would not be undertaking any future winter tours so that he could build up business in his sports shop, England were left with a massive void to fill.

In view of the patience he had shown for many years as Knott's understudy, Taylor, by then aged forty, fully deserved to spend two years as England's undisputed first-choice wicket-keeper. But all the time the selectors made it abundantly clear that they were searching for another Knott, casting envious eyes at the West Indians who had unearthed the dual talents of Jeff Dujon. Lord's dabbled with a variety of names including Ian Gould from Sussex, David Bairstow of Yorkshire and Middlesex's Paul Downton, without achieving the desired effect. In Australia in the winter of 1986–87, as Mike Gatting's team swept all before them, Surrey's Jack Richards appeared to provide the answer, scoring 133 on only his second Test appearance at Perth. But his batting failed to reach the same heights again and he was dropped the following summer after playing one Test against Pakistan. At the end of 1988 he announced his premature retirement from the game after a contractual dispute with his county.

Around the seventeen first-class counties there was no shortage of young wicket-keepers attempting to catch the selectors' eyes, but not so many were offering the added advantage of runs and, as England's manager Micky Stewart said, 'If a side has a wicket-keeper who is a capable batsman then it is going to have far more potential in terms of balance.'

Jack Russell shows the fierce determination that earned him his maiden first-class century against the Aussies at Old Trafford . . .

After England's two planned tours for the winter of 1988–89 to India and New Zealand were cancelled for political reasons, Stewart and the new chairman of selectors, Ted Dexter, had some difficulty deciding who should stand behind the stumps for the 1989 home clashes with Australia. For the one-day internationals at the end of May they went for Worcestershire's Steve Rhodes, who had won England 'B' caps in Sri Lanka four years earlier and who had scored valuable runs the previous summer as the West Midlands side won the County Championship. But for the first of the Ashes Tests they opted for Jack Russell of Gloucestershire who, for several seasons, had been outstanding with the gloves but who had been held back by his lack of runs.

The critics, particularly former England captain Tony Greig, were not impressed with Russell at Headingley where, batting at nine in the order behind all-rounders Derek Pringle and Phil Newport, he made 15 and as England slumped to defeat by 210 runs. He looked particularly in trouble against the raw pace of Merv Hughes, and there was considerable argument in favour of reverting to Rhodes for the second game at Lord's.

But Russell, a slim, determined West Countryman, was not going to surrender his long-awaited Test place without a fight, and went to Stewart for help. The manager recalled:

> Jack's batting at Leeds had not pleased him. He got a lot of stick in the media for the way he hadn't coped with the shorter-pitched deliveries and so we set out to put it right. We worked on what balls he should play and those that should be left alone. We told him to play straight rather than try to work the ball square of the wicket and we impressed upon him the importance of keeping his back foot planted firmly on the ground instead of hopping around at the crease.
>
> He said he had difficulty picking up the shorter balls so we started a series of exercises that began with us lobbing the ball at his head – gently – from close range, then gradually moving further away and whizzing it at him. Although there wasn't a lot of time, he practised hard and also was aware that he had to adopt a more positive approach. That didn't mean hitting out at every ball, it was more a case of showing the bowlers that he was not prepared to be dominated.

The difference in Russell's batting was amazing when the two sides met for a second time at Lord's. As England's morale sunk lower against an underrated (but proving highly effective) Australian pace attack, he top-scored with 64 not out in the first innings, scoring nine fours and baiting Hughes who, despite taking four for 71, found he could not 'bounce out' a player who had been considered his bunny two weeks earlier. And if the critics needed any convincing that Russell was a reformed character he provided further evidence with 29 in the second innings before England lost by six wickets and 42 in the weather-ravaged Third Test at Edgbaston.

But it was in the fourth contest at Old Trafford, as the roof was threatening to cave in on England, that Russell, who had been promoted on merit to bat at seven following Ian Botham, provided the big innings that ensured he would figure in the selectors' minds for some time to come.

England's first-innings batting at Manchester followed what was becoming a fairly familiar pattern, as Geoff Lawson quickly had the Aussies in total command with the wickets of Graham Gooch, Tim Curtis and Tim Robinson. Among his six victims was also Russell, trapped lbw for 1, and it was only a brilliant maiden Test century from Robin Smith and a late 39 from Neil Foster that enabled England to reach 260.

There was little flamboyance about the Australian reply, as Allan Border's highly efficient outfit knew that with a two–nil lead in the six-match series, another victory would clinch the Ashes while a draw would leave England struggling at dormie two down. Half-centuries from Border, Mark Taylor, Steve Waugh and Dean Jones were sufficient to build up a score of 447 and a lead of 187.

England's second innings began inside the first hour on the Monday of the Test and within ninety minutes it became obvious that another crushing defeat was on the cards. While Lawson had been the first-day destroyer, he handed over the executioner's sword to Terry Alderman and with his unerring line, length and late swing England were struggling.

Although Gooch took 10 off Lawson's first over, Curtis was fortunate to survive a very confident appeal for leg before from the first ball by Alderman and was caught at short leg off the second. Robinson struggled for twenty-eight balls before he played across the line and was lbw, and Gooch had made only 13 when he edged Lawson into the hands of Alderman, who was resting between overs at slips. Worse still followed for England, as Smith followed an

Alderman delivery down the leg side and was caught behind, Botham was trapped lbw and in no time at all Gower was caught in the gully off Lawson to leave his side in the cart at 59 for 6. Relief for the beleaguered home side arrived only at tea in the form of heavy rain, but there was still the fifth day to be negotiated.

The mood in the England camp could hardly have been lower when they started on the final day. At breakfast the players had learnt through the *Today* newspaper that sixteen English cricketers had signed up to take part in a rebel tour to South Africa the following winter – a story that was to be confirmed within hours by a statement issued from Johannesburg. Among the defectors were John Emburey and Neil Foster, upon whose shoulders rested much of England's hopes of saving the game.

Whatever his future allegiances, Emburey – having been informed that England did not plan to pick any of the rebels in any of the remaining games of the series – made it abundantly clear that he intended to make his exit from official Test cricket on a high note. And with Russell improving as a batsman with almost every innings he played, the Aussies were made to fight hard for the Ashes.

It was well after lunch when Alderman brought the ball back off the pitch to hit Emburey's off stump, and by then the Middlesex man had made 64, the seventh-wicket stand had raised 142 and England were at least spared the embarrassment of defeat by an innings. The stand was only one short of the English seventh-wicket record for the Ashes, and Russell had contributed fully. The nervous nudges, so apparent at Leeds, had disappeared. In their place was a series of confident drives sprinkled with the odd powerful pull over mid-wicket.

Foster showed just as much dedication in his last Test as Emburey, keeping Russell company for half an hour as the wicket-keeper moved ever closer to the maiden first-class century that would cement his place in the side. There was added support from Gus Fraser, which gave England hope that a match once beyond redemption could be saved. However, when the last man Nick Cook was caught behind off the bowling of Hughes, the Australians were left needing only 78 to win to become the first side to regain the Ashes in England for fifty-five years. They duly received that target for the loss of only one wicket, and England were left to reminisce on Russell's gallant effort. The wicket-keeper, who many had said could

. . . and receives well-earned congratulations from sporting Aussie skipper Allan Border

not bat, had defied the Australians for 320 minutes, facing 260 balls and scoring fourteen crisp fours in his undefeated 128. It was an innings of much grit and determination and England could only regret that many of the so-called front-line batsmen had displayed less than half of his tenacity.

As Stewart said later: 'The remarkable thing about Jack's innings was the way he used everything he had practised and also the way in which he kept going. It is always hard to score a hundred, but even harder when you are not used to batting with such concentration over a long period.' Stewart also revealed that during their coaching he had been helped in some sessions by Knott, who had become a 'wicket-keeping adviser' to the England selection committee. The master from the past had certainly helped to fashion a chip off the old block.